The

FOOTSTEPS

of

Divine Providence

August Hermann Francke

ISBN (print):   978-1-952139-24-6
ISBN (Kindle): 978-1-952139-23-9

Publication arranged by Pioneer Library
Publisher of classic missions and devotional books

CONTENTS

.

FOREWORD (2021)

HISTORIAN David Bebbington famously defines evangelicalism using four distinctive elements: biblicism, cross-centeredness, conversionism, and activism. This potent blend is frequently traced back to John Wesley, whose heart was "strangely warmed" by a personal conversion at Aldersgate Street in 1738. But we can see most, if not all, of the evangelical distinctives at work in the German Pietists who preceded and directly influenced the Wesleys .

August Hermann Francke (1663-1727), the writer of the present book, was a key figure in the emergence of Pietism. Along with Philipp Jakob Spener, he founded the "Collegium Philobiblicum" for reading the Scriptures in the original languages on Sunday afternoons. A number of college students were brought to a living faith while studying the Scriptures with Spener and Francke. In addition to extending Bible knowledge and supporting overseas evangelism, Francke also supported a wide variety of charitable works through his foundations in Halle. In him the mind of the scholar and the heart of compassion dwelt with no contradiction.

Francke cherished a deep regard for both testaments of the Bible. He was determined to thoroughly acquaint himself with the biblical languages. During his studies at Erfurt, he read the Hebrew Bible through seven times in a single year. He graduated and was appointed Privatdozent at Leipzig in 1685. He held numerous lectures to offer biblical education. encouraging Germans to read the Bible for themselves. The practice of individual, devotional reading of the Bible was a trend that could only begin in earnest after the invention of Gutenberg's printing press; the Pietists were among its greatest promoters.

In 1690, Francke was prohibited from lecturing in Leipzig due to his Pietist views—namely, his focus on individual conversion and personal Bible reading. He returned to Erfurt with an opportunity to minister. He was asked to translate a work by Miguel de Molinos, a controversial Spanish mystic, and accepted. After just fifteen months, this work gained him a number of detractors, and on September 27, 1691, he was commanded to leave Erfurt as well.

When the University of Halle was founded in 1694, Francke was given the chair of Greek and Oriental languages. The university was founded by

FOREWORD

Frederick III, Elector of Brandenburg.[1] Frederick III would be an important patron through much of August Francke's life. Seven years later, Frederick III became King Frederick I of Prussia. He helped to make Halle something of a haven for German Pietists like Spener and Francke.

Not longer after Francke came to Halle, in 1695, he reached a conviction to support several orphans, beyond his ability, trusting God to support the work. As this charitable work continued to grow, in 1698, Francke received 100,000 bricks from Frederick III to create a permanent boarding house—called a "hospital" in the English of the time. This boarding house supported not only orphans, but needy children more generally, as is made clear in the narrative that follows. It was granted a legal charter by Frederick III in September 1698.

In 1701, Francke began the work of setting up an dispensary. This was finished in the summer, and in the autumn a printing house was completed as well. With the founding of the pharmacy and printing house, what was only a boarding house became a multifaceted institution that took up a short street in Halle, now known as the Francke Foundations. These foundations wielded tremendous influence on the Protestantism of the day.

---

[1] The University of Halle was merged with the University of Wittenberg in 1817 and became part of the University of Halle-Wittenberg, now Martin Luther University of Halle-Wittenberg.

Numerous theological works by Francke and others were put into circulation.[2] It is difficult to imagine the influence of such a printing house in the early eighteenth century. From 1687 to the time of his death in 1727, over 2000 works appear in library catalogues with Francke credited as an author, editor, or publisher. Many of these were brief newsletters or sermons; this figure also includes Bibles and theological works in German, Dutch, Swedish, French, Italian, Latin, Greek, Hungarian, Czech, and Arabic. More than a million Bibles were printed and distributed by the Francke Foundations.

Francke was also a key figure in the beginnings of Protestant missions outside of Europe. When King Frederick IV of Denmark decided to found a Christian mission in his colony at Tranquebar, one of his court preachers asked Francke to recruit from among his students in Halle. Francke recruited Bartholomäus Ziegenbalg and Henry Plütschau from among his students, and they arrived in Tranquebar on July 6, 1706. While they were overseas, Francke supported them by printing their newsletters in Halle. When he died in 1727, his son carried on the work of the Francke Foundations, which continued to operate until 1946 when the

---

[2] You can see the original editions in the Francke Portal at the Franckesche Stiftungen website, which has more than 16,000 documents, around half of which are digitized: http://digital.francke-halle.de/fsfp

FOREWORD

Soviet presidium abolished the Foundations. Some of the buildings still stand, and the site has been on the German proposal list to become a UNESCO World Heritage site.

In spite of his many contributions to Protestant theology and practice, very little has been published in recent times about August Francke. In the eighteenth and ninteenth centuries, A long article, "August Hermann Francke and His Work" (1897), was written by Marie E. Richard and has been made available by Pioneer Library in digital format. Gary R. Sattler has written *God's Glory, Neighbor's Good: A Brief Introduction to the Life and Writings of August Hermann Francke* (1982) is long out of print and difficult to obtain.

The following autobiographical account of August Hermann Francke's charitable work was first printed in separate installments in German. It was translated into English in 1705 under the title *Pietas Hallensis*. The 1705 edition included an appendix, which included a miscellany of letters and directions pertaining to Francke's Foundations.

This edition is based on that of 1787, which includes an uncredited introduction. The original spelling and punctuation have been kept, and all footnotes are reproduced from 1787 edition except for those that bear the initials of the present editor.

M.S.

v

THE

F O O T S T E P S

OF

Divine Providence;

OR, THE

BOUNTIFUL HAND of HEAVEN

DEFRAYING THE

EXPENCES OF FAITH:

Wonderfully displayed in erecting and managing the

H O S P I T A L

AT

GLAUCHA WITHOUT HALL,

IN THE

PRUSSIAN DOMINIONS,

FOR THE EDUCATION OF

STUDENTS IN DIVINITY;

AND FOR THE

RECEPTION, CLOATHING, FEEDING, AND EDUCATING

OF

POOR CHILDREN.

Carried on by the instrumentality of that humble, and blessed Servant of GOD,

AUGUSTUS HERMANNUS FRANCK.

Except the LORD build the House, they labor in vain that built it.
Psalm cxxvii. 1.
Length of Days is in her right Hand; and in her left Hand, Riches and Honor.
Prov. iii. 16.

Here the title page to the 1787 edition is reproduced.

INTRODUCTION

TO

PROFESSOR FRANCK's BOOK

ON THE

Footsteps of Providence;

IN WHICH IS

Demonstrated the Existence, Perfections, and Providence of GOD, from the Principles of Reason and Revelation.

I. THE EXISTENCE OF GOD.

THE constitution of man, his perceptive powers and inward sense, *i.e.* his moral sense, are so framed, that he can no sooner open the eyes of his body and mind, and think like a man, but he discerns the glory of his omnipotent Maker: his reason must as naturally conclude, that the highest veneration ought to be given to infinite Majesty, the strongest affection to infinite Goodness, the greatest fear to infinite Power, and the firmest obedience to infinite Dominion; and that it must be the best and noblest improvement of human nature, to resemble the truth, justice, purity and beneficence of GOD, which is the sum and substance of religion.

II. So that Religion is as true as our faculties; for if there is such a thing as reason, there is such a Being as a GOD. Therefore it is scarcely imaginable that a man, in the right use of his perceptive powers, and inward sense, can be a steady and persevering atheist; for there are five demonstrations of a God ever before his eyes.

1. The admirable frame and structure of the visible universe.

2. The manifold footsteps of an over-ruling Providence.

3. The reasonable sentiments of all sober men in all ages.

4. The wonderful frame and contexture of our own bodies.

5. The divine faculties and sublime operations of our souls.

The grand, original, fundamental law of nature, is founded on this self-evident axiom, or maxim of truth, THAT NOTHING CAN GIVE TO ANOTHER WHAT IT HAS NOT IN ITSELF TO GIVE. From this a man may easily infer, that all the goodness, life, power and intelligence diffused through the creatures, must be found, in an eminent way, collected in the uncreated, self-existent mind of GOD, who must therefore be possessed of all possible perfection; and if so, he must be a GOD of truth; and if a GOD of truth, it must be his will that man should not form any false conceptions of his divine nature. And hence the first law of nature is this, that man should believe the existence of GOD, and should entertain the most honorable idea of Him, that his understanding can possibly conceive: that he should acknowledge and extol his divine attributes, and revere his supreme dignity and incomprehensible excellence: that he should own, magnify and adore his unspeakable glory and majesty—contemplate with admiration and rapture his boundless perfections—bow down his soul in low submission to his sovereign greatness—praise and exalt, with the most ardent strains of devotion, his all-sufficiency, and independent self-existence: that he should stand in awe of his dreadful and irresistible power—express the highest love of his essential goodness—constantly observe and regard, with deep veneration, his presence in all places, and attentively advert to his unlimited knowledge, who not only takes notice of all our actions, but searches the secrets of the heart, views the bent and inclination of the soul, and sees our thoughts and purposes, even at their first ebullition, and imperfect eruption from the mind.

PROVIDENCE is nothing less than the omnipresent mind of the eternal SON of GOD, preserving and governing his own world.

The LORD JESUS produced the universe by an act of his will, which before that act had no existence. He upholds the whole world every moment, or it would fall into ruins. He actuates and enlivens the creation, otherwise it would be a lifeless mass. He

3

recovered it from the curse, when man had forfeited all into the hands of Divine Justice, by his treason and rebellion against the majesty, dominion, and dignity of GOD.

He preserves and governs all creatures, according to their different natures; as, dead matter—vegetable substances—animal bodies—and rational immortal minds.

He preserves and governs dead matter by his own grand law of gravitation. He preserves and governs vegetable bodies, according to the laws of attraction and nutrition, which he made for them. He preserves and governs all animal bodies, of birds, beasts, fishes, reptiles, and insects, by giving them the great law of instinct and genius, or aptitude for their peculiar kinds of action, which they every moment perform. He preserves and governs all mankind, by the law he has impressed upon the human nature. This law is the will of CHRIST, grounded in the nature, constitution, and powers of man, commanding what is right, and forbidding what is wrong.

Having demonstrated the existence and perfections of GOD, let us now evince the existence of a special Providence, exercised by the LORD JESUS towards his peculiar people, through every period of their lives; who is attentive to all their most minute circumstances.

The Scripture evidences of a peculiar Providence, pour in upon us like the tides of the ocean; or the beams of light from the sun, which dart every way through a vast expanse of thousands of millions of miles, with excessive brightness and beauty. The abundance of proofs, makes it an arduous work to arrange and display them in proper order. Let us try at the most clear and easy methods of demonstration, so that each head of evidence may enlighten the understanding, convince the conscience, impress the memory, charm the affections, and regulate our life and conversation. The glorious Being of GOD—the boundless perfections of the Divine Nature of JESUS CHRIST —the structure of the visible world, and its astonishing preservation—the beauty, order, and elegance of the universe—the amazing blessings of GOD bestowed on the whole world of mankind— the awful judgments of GOD upon many daring sinners— and the fears and terrors of guilty minds: all these evince a Providence. To which may be added, the glaring absurdities, and ruinous consequences, which arise and flow from a denial of the special Providence that preserves and governs the world.

But we have yet more striking and comfortable evidences of the peculiar Providence of CHRIST over all his redeemed people.

I. ANSWERS to PRAYER, a convincing EVIDENCE of a special PROVIDENCE.

1. Abraham's servant prays—Rebekah appears. Gen. xxiv. 15.

2. Jacob wrestles with God—Esau's heart is softened. Gen. xxxiii. 10.
3. Moses prays—the Red Sea divides. Exod. xiv. 15.
4. Moses lifts up his hands—Israel ruins the Amalekites. Exod. xvii. 11.
5. Hannah prays—Samuel is given. 1 Sam. i. 27.
6. Manoah prays—JESUS appears. Judges xiii. 9.
7. David prays—Ahithophel hangs himself. 2 Sam. xv. 31.
8. Asa prays—a victory is gained over a million of men. 2 Chron. xiv. 11.
9. Elijah prays—the heavens are brass. 1 Kings xvii. 1.
10. Elijah cries to GOD—the heavens pour down floods. 1 Kings xviii. 1.
11. Elijah prays—fire descends on the sacrifice. 1 Kings xviii. 36.
12. Elijah prays—fire burns an hundred men. 2 Kings i. 12.
13. Jehoshaphat prays to GOD—and is immediately saved from death. 1 Kings xxii. 32. 2 Chron xviii. 31.
14. Hezekiah prays—and 185,000 men are struck dead in one night. 2 Kings xix. 14. Isai. xxxvii. 16.
15. Hezekiah prays—the sun goes back. Isai. xxxviii. 5.
16. Three heroes pray—fire is turned into frost. Dan. iii. 17.

17. Daniel prays—the grand dream is revealed. Dan. ii. 18.

18. Daniel prays—lions are made lambs. Dan. vi. 22.

19. Daniel prays—seventy weeks are revealed. Dan. ix. 2, 3.

20. Esther prays—Haman is hanged. Esth. iv. 16.

21. Ezra prays—GOD answers in a moment. Ezra. viii. 21-23.

22. Nehemiah prays—the king's heart is turned. Neh. ii. 4.

23. Jonah prays at the bottom of the sea, and the belly of hell—he rises, and is safe on dry land. Jonah ii. 2.

24. Gideon prays—the fleece is wet. Judg. vi. 37, 38.——He prays again—the fleece is dry. Ver. 40.

25. The Church of CHRIST prays—Peter's prison doors fly open. Acts xii. 5-7.

REMARKS

See the omnipotent Powers, and glorious Victory of PRAYER!

Prayer has saved kingdoms—made armies victorious—removed terrible judgments—brought down millions of blessings—delivered multitudes of single believers—stopped the sun in his race, and the moon in her course—quenches the flames of fire—muzzled a den of lions—divided the raging seas—driven out legions of devils—brought back immortal souls from the eternal world—and conquered the eternal GOD himself, the great and immortal JEHOVAH.

II. CRITICAL TIMES *of* DISTRESS; *or the Appearance of* GOD *the* REDEEMER *in the Pinches of Providence.*

JEHOVAH-JIREH—*the LORD will provide.*

1. Abraham lifts up his knife to cut Isaac's throat —the Messenger JEHOVAH appears. Gen. xxii. 10, 11.

2. Lot on the point of ruin—the angel pulls him into safety. Gen. xix. 10.

3. Hagar and Ishmael dying with thirst—a well appears. Gen. xvi. 13. xxi. 19.

4. Rebekah comes to the well in the very moment Abraham's steward was looking for direction. Gen. xxiv. 15.

5. The Midianites merchant-men appear, and Joseph is saved from death. Gen. xxxvii. 28.

6. Joseph interprets the butler's dream, and that butler is forced, after vile neglect, to bring Joseph into Pharaoh's presence, who advances him to honor, power and glory. Gen xli. 9-46.

7. The famine forces Jacob to send into Egypt for corn; this brings on the most happy discovery of his beloved son Joseph, and his own future safety from ruin. Gen. xlii. xlv.——That man must be worse

than the devil, who will not acknowledge the footsteps of GOD in this affair!

8. The infant Moses on the brink of ruin among the flags of the river Nile—Pharaoh's daughter appears to save him. Exod. ii. 2-6.

9. Moses flees from the wrath of the king—Jethro provides for his safety forty years. Exod. ii. 15, 16.

10. Moses steps into the sea—that moment the waters divide. Exod. xiv. 15.

11. Sisera flees into Jael's tent—he is nailed to the floor, and the Israelites are saved from ruin. Judg. iv. 18.

12. Ruth in poverty is forced to glean corn—Boaz appears, makes her his wife, and the owner of all his vast estate. Ruth ii. 3, 4.

13. Goliath, the Philistine bully, insults GOD and his people—David, a shepherd boy, appears with a sling and a stone, brings the monster to the ground, and cuts off his head. 1 Sam. xvii. 50.

14. David escapes death from a javelin, by the quickness of his eye, directed by Providence. 1 Sam. xviii. 11. xix. 9, 10.

15. The Philistines invade the land of Israel that moment Saul is on the point of killing David. 1 Sam. xxiii. 26, 27.

16. David, by means of a fainting Egyptian, recovers his beloved Abigail, and all the plunder of Ziklag. 1 Sam. xxx. 11-18.

9

17. A man draws a bow at a venture—the wicked Ahab is slain, and Elijah is saved from his enemy. 1 Kings xxii. 30.

18. The waters appear as blood to the army of Moabites—they are led into a snare, and the Israelites gain the victory. 2 Kings iii. 23, 24.

19. Rabshakeh vows vengeance on Hezekiah, and daringly defies and blasphemes GOD; and that night the insolent atheist, with his army of 185,000 men, are struck dead, and Sennacherib murdered by his own sons. 2 Kings xix. 35. 2 Chron. xxxii. 21. Isaiah xxxvii. 36.

20. Haman forms a wicked plot to destroy all the Jews; he casts lots for a prosperous day—the lot fell eleven months distant. Esther iii. 7.

21. Haman erects a gallows to hang Mordecai—that night the king could not sleep: Mordecai is exalted, and Haman hanged. Esther vi. 1-4. vii. 9.

22. Forty men swear they will kill Paul—the chief captain prevents the plot. Acts xxiii. 12.

23. The silent, invisible, but powerful energy of CHRIST's Providence, sways the heart of Festus the prevent a second plot against Paul's life. Acts xxv. 3, 4.

24. Paul, in a dreadful storm, is saved, with all the crew in the ship. Acts xxvii. 43, 44.

III. GOD *the* REDEEMER *has acted above, beyond or contrary to his* Laws *of* Nature, *for the* Preservation *and* Salvation *of his People*.

Witness Noah in the deluge: the Israelites at the Red Sea: the manna sent for forty years, and the rock flowing with water. Witness the river of Jordan, and the walls of Jericho. Witness the sun and moon: the strength of Sampson: the supernatural valor of David: the ruin of Sennacherib's army: the burning fiery furnace: the den of roaring lions: the monstrous fish that vomited Jonah on dry land: with ten thousand other wonders, which we are unable to enumerate.

IV. *An* Association *of* natural *and* moral Causes.

Causes have been ordered, directed and actuated by the omnipresent REDEEMER, for the preservation, deliverance and success of his people. In the history of Joseph we have ten or twelve steps of Providence, all tending to his advancement to honor and power; and if one link in the grand chain of Providence had failed, all would have failed, and come to nothing. And in the preservation and advancement of Esther to the throne, and of Mordecai to be the first man, next the king, in one hundred and twenty-seven provinces, you must be blind as a stone, if you do not see the agency of GOD our SAVIOUR. The reader may easily add Moses and David, with many others, to the number.

THE FOOTSTEPS OF DIVINE PROVIDENCE

V. Kindnesses done to GOD's People, have been
generously rewarded, and Injuries offered to them
have been most dreadfully punished, by the Justice
of the LORD JESUS, in every Age of the World.

GOD blessed, not only the house of Potiphar, but all
the kingdom of Egypt, for the sake of Joseph, Gen.
xxxix. 5. as He had before done to Laban, for the
sake of his servant Jacob. Gen. xxx. 27.

The Egyptian midwives saved the children of the
Israelites from the bloody cruelty of Pharaoh; and
GOD built them houses, *i.e.* preserved and blessed
their families. Exod. i. 20, 21.

Rahab hid the spies, and GOD the REDEEMER
saved all her house from destruction. Josh. vii. 17.

Obed-edom entertained the ark, and the blessing
of GOD came down upon all his house. 2 Sam. vi.
11, 12.

In all ages, families, cities, and kingdoms, have
been blessed for the sake of the righteous; and ten
good men would have been the preservation of four
cities from fire and brimstone. Gen. xviii. 32.

On the other hand, you see that tyrant, the king
of Egypt, drowns the infants in the river Nile, and
Justice drowns him, and all his host, in the Red Sea.
Exod. xiv. 28.

King Saul flings a javelin to kill righteous David;
and Justice leaves the tyrant to fall upon his own
sword. 1 Sam. xviii. 10. xix. 10. xxxi. 4.

The wicked noblemen in Darius's court contrive to have Daniel thrown into the lion's den—the vengeance of GOD causes the lions to break their bones, before they come to the bottom of it. Dan. vi. 24.

Ahab spills Naboth's blood—the dogs lick Ahab's blood on the very same spot. 1 Kings xxi. 19. xxii. 38.

Jeroboam stretches out his hand to seize a prophet —that hand and arm are instantly struck dead. 1 Kings xiii. 4.

Elymas opposes Paul, and he is struck blind in a moment. Acts xiii. 10, 11.

On the other hand, Publius and his friends, at Malta, shew kindness to Paul; and his house, and the whole island, are the better for it. Acts xxvii. 7-9.

In all ages GOD the REDEEMER has made good that promise, copied from his heart, I will bless them that bless thee; and that threatening, copied from his wrath, I will curse them that curse thee. Gen. xii. 2, 3.

VI. *The* Prevention *of Sin in good Men and bad Men, is a striking Evidence of the special Providence of* GOD.

GOD says to Abimelech, I withheld thee from sinning against me. Gen. xx. 6.

David was kept from commiting [*sic*] a most rash and dreadful murder by Divine Providence. 1 Sam. xxv. 33.

Wicked resolutions to murder the apostle Paul, were defeated twice, yea, *three times!* Acts xxi. 31. xxiii. 21. xxv. 3.

These are astonishing proofs of the ever active understanding, omnipresence, almighty power, and faithfulness of the LORD JESUS CHRIST!

Thus, my dear reader, you see these striking evidences of the existence, attributes, and special Providence of GOD our SAVIOUR: and the following narrative of that incomparable man of GOD, Professor *Franck*, is a most glorious exemplification of these evidences of Divine Providence.

All places are full of GOD; all nature is his habitation, all space his abode. The sun and moon, and every star, points us to a GOD: the air, earth, and seas, proclaim the wisdom, power, and agency of GOD. Every plant, tree and flower, every bird, beast, fish and insect, proclaims a GOD. Not the least stick or straw, but tells us there is a GOD: not the least breath or whisper of air, but would sound as loud as thunder in our ears, the wisdom and goodness of GOD, if our hearts were not poisoned with atheism and enmity against Him.

But such an eminent believer as Professor *Franck* was not contented with mere rational and philosophical views of the being and perfections of GOD. He was assisted by the ETERNAL SPIRIT to view every thing in that point of light in which it is placed by DIVINE REVELATION: and this taught him to see all things in heaven, earth, and hell, in the immediate hands, and under the intire dominion of the only LORD GOD; or, as the original Greek ought to be translated, the only SOVEREIGN MASTER, and GOD and LORD of us, JESUS CHRIST. Jude, ver. 4. *Kai ton monon Despoteen Theon kai Kurion emoon Iesoun Christon.*³ This great and good Professor *Franck* saw CHRIST in every creature, and saw every creature to be nothing without CHRIST. He had a realizing faith in JEHOVAH JESUS, and this led him to scorn and abhor all those corrupt and false ideas of the person of CHRIST, which represent Him as a *created God*, or a *mere man* like ourselves, born from the conjunction of Joseph and his wife, in the same manner as all other men are. ——No, Sirs; Dr. *Franck* durst not give the lye direct to the ETERNAL SPIRIT, and GOD the FATHER likewise; who assure us, that GOD should perform *a new thing in the earth:* such a new thing as never was before, and will never be again. *Jer.* xxxi. 22. *Ki harah* JEHOVAH *chadasha baaretz neckabah tesobeb gaber.*⁴

The HOLY GHOST *shall come upon thee.* Luke i. 35. *He,* i.e. Joseph, *knew her not till she had brought forth her first-born son, and he called his name JESUS.* Matt. i. 21. This is the positive testimony of the GOD of truth;

---

³ The text is given here without transliteration: καὶ τὸν μόνον δεσπότην Θεόν, καὶ κύριον ἡμῶν Ἰησοῦν Χριστὸν. (M.S.)

⁴ The Masoretic Text of this verse reads, כִּי־בָרָא יְהוָה חֲדָשָׁה בָּאָרֶץ נְקֵבָה תְּסוֹבֵב גָּבֶר. (M.S.)

to which *Socinians* reply, that the HOLY SPIRIT is a grand liar, and that GOD the FATHER has set his seal to the most notorious lye that ever was declared in the world.[5]

But Dr. *Franck* believed just the reverse of all this impudence and blasphemy: he knew that GOD our SAVIOUR fills heaven and earth: that He is no temporary God by office, but EXISTS ALL AT ONCE, from eternity to eternity: he found Him to be an omnipresent Friend—ever living with him—ever living in him, as the only Spring and Source of his life, as the great Pattern of his life, and the sole End of his existence and immortal powers: he found CHRIST to be the Life of his understanding, of his will, memory, conscience and affections: he found CHRIST to be the Life of his faith, and *he was strong in faith*, giving glory to the perfections of his GOD and SAVIOUR.

---

[5] Joseph Priestly, L.L.D. in his fourth letter to the Jews, page 40, 41, has the unparalleled boldness to declare, before GOD and the whole world, "The history of the miraculous conception of JESUS, does not appear to me to be sufficiently authenticated.—Your sacred books, as well as ours, being written by *men*, neither of them can be expected to be intirely free from mistakes, or exempt from interpolations.

"Myself, and many other Christians, are not believers in the MIRACULOUS CONCEPTION OF JESUS, but are of opinion, that he was the LEGITIMATE SON OF JOSEPH."

GOD the ETERNAL SPIRIT gave him a confident expectation of things hoped for, and the convincing evidence of invisible transactions. *Heb.* xi. 1. He realized the invisible Persons of FATHER, SON, and HOLY SPIRIT—he realized the invisible transactions of the *SACRED THREE*, in their purposes and councils concerning our salvation—he realized the invisible blessings contained in all the exceeding great and precious promises. 2 Pet. i. 4.

He had a full confidence in GOD's sincerity and faithfulness, with respect to the fulfillment of all the promises: he had a full persuasion that GOD would be true to his soul, and to his own promises.

He had a fixed and strong rational persuasion powerfully working in his soul, which carried him above all frightful discouragements, and terrifying outward appearances of things. GOD the incarnate REDEEMER was his inexhaustible bank of riches: in Him he found immense stores of goodness and grace, mercy and love; and he had a bold intrepid claim to all the bank stock of GOD for himself, as his own real eternal portion and possession: and, for the great and lasting happiness of all Germany, he had a *claiming faith* for the continual carrying on of that great design of the Orphan-house, which has now subsisted near ninety-two years. And we may justly conclude that many hundreds of thousands, if not millions, have been comforted from his experience, which GOD gave him to be the instrument of such immense good to the Church, and the world!

Note in 1787 edition:

Most adorable and ever-present GOD and SAVIOUR! we see thy eternal power and Godhead in this grand affair, from the first moment till this very day: it was thy hand that formed this great and good man: thou didst give him his strong natural powers: thou didst inspire him with a noble genius for learning and the sciences: thou didst enable him to attain all the embellishments of his mind and understanding, and thou didst give him higher accomplishments than all the beauties of the sciences. Thou wast the sole Author, Object, Feeder and Finisher of his faith: thou was the Author, the Object, and the Feeder of his love. He loved Thee with a vast admiration and esteem, with a boundless benevolence and gratitude: he thought of Thee as the most worthy and beautiful Person: he desired thy presence as the life of his soul: he bore the strongest good-will to thine interest and kingdom in the immortal souls of men: he delighted in Thee as the eternal and immutable Truth and Beauty, and he rejoiced in Thee as the Ocean of all his happiness for time and eternity!

O, my dear reader! do you not ardently pray to our good GOD and SAVIOUR, to make you resemble this great and holy man? Do you not see, and long to imitate him in his faith, and bold claims upon his best and eternal Friend? Do you not see his noble and fixed dependence on the uprightness, sincerity, veracity and faithfulness of CHRIST, pledged in his promises, sealed by his blood, and confirmed by his tremendous oath, and the eternal deposit of the HOLY SPIRIT in his heart? This gave him a full, unshaken confidence, and intrepid expectation, that he never should be confounded or ashamed: that nothing should disappoint his hopes, or damp his joys: that all dark Providences should work for his good; all apparent losses should increase his riches; and all seeming crosses should make his comforts grow, and his pleasures in CHRIST abound. Is not his experience desirable? I am sure it is. Where that is, there is an ardent desire that the man's bitterest enemies may partake of the same joys. True Grace is the most generous principle in the world: it teaches and animates the souls of believers to seek the peace of every place where they live, and to make every one the wiser, better, and happier, with whom they have the least connexion, or over whom they have the least influence. Do you feel this public spirit strongly working in your soul? Do you wish to see the kingdom of Great Britain flourish, not only in arts and commerce, in pasturage and husbandry, but in science and learning, in virtue and good manners: but much higher than all these, in the fear of GOD: in a veneration for his ever-active presence and boundless perfections: in a strict regard for the honor of his Name, and the acknowledgment of his attributes: in gratitude for the infinite advantages of Divine Revelation, even to the common understanding and reason of mankind; and information in the true foundations of moral virtue; such are prudence, justice, temperance and fortitude?

But higher still. Do you feel public spirit for the Church of CHRIST in this country? Do you love to see the Divine Life and Godlike Nature, the Image of CHRIST and the Power of Godliness, flourish in the souls of GOD's beloved and chosen people?

Do you wish to see all the graces of GOD's HOLY SPIRIT rise into the most blooming perfection of beauty, in their exercise towards CHRIST, the FATHER, the HOLY SPIRIT, and all mankind: teaching us at the same moment *to deny all ungodliness and worldly lusts, and to live soberly* in self-government, as well as *righteously* in the exercise of every branch of moral justice, *and godly, in this present* EVIL WORLD?

Do you wish to see the Gospel rise above its present banks and bounds, and swell like a mighty flood, and spread all round the world from pole to pole?

Do you wish to see the poor, blind, miserable Jews, made to know JESUS, the true GOD, and eternal Life?

Dr. AUGUSTUS HERMANNUS FRANCK, was born at Lubeck, in Germany, on the 12th of March, in the year 1663.—His father was Mr. John Franck, a counsellor at law; and his mother Ann, was daughter of Mr. David Gloxin, senior, burgomaster of Lubeck. He was educated at the universities of Erfurt, Leipsick, and Luneberg; and began to preach at Luneburg in the year 1687. He settled at Glaucha, in the suburbs of the city of Hall, in Saxonhy, in the year 1694. He began his grand design of the Orphan-house and College for students in divinity, at East 1695.

☞ *Speedily will be published the LIFE and CHARACTER at* LARGE *of Dr.* FRANCK, *by W. JUSTINS*, No 35, SHOEMAKER-ROW, BLACKFRIARS, *near* LUDGATE-HILL, APRIL 25, 1787.

P.S. See Dr. Woodward's Boylean Lectures, and Sir Richard Blackmore on the Law of Nature.

A striking passage against Socinians was omitted in its proper place. Isa. vii. 14. *Hinneh haolmeh harah vejoledeth ben vekarat shemo Gnim-anu-el.*[6] "Behold! a virgin shall be pregnant, and bring forth a Son; and thou shalt call his name IMM-ANU-EL—GOD with us."

---

[6] In the Masoretic Text, the verse reads הִנֵּה הָעַלְמָה הָרָה וְיֹלֶדֶת בֵּן וְקָרֵאת שְׁמוֹ עִמָּנוּ אֵל. (M.S.)

AN
ACCOUNT
OF THE MOST REMARKABLE
FOOTSTEPS
OF
Divine Providence,
IN THE
ERECTING and MANAGING the HOSPITAL at
GLAUCHA without HALL.

INTRODUCTION:
Containing the Reasons and Motives of the present Narrative.
1. Whereas his Royal Prussian Majesty and Electoral Highness of Brandenburgh, *Frederick* I. was in the year 1700 graciously pleased to inform himself, in the exactest manner possible, concerning the Hospital, and the whole method there contrived for the better educating and cultivating of youth, at Glaucha without Hall; and this by the care and management of four of his honorable Privy Council: and whereas after they had not only taken a strict survey of all particulars relating to this affair, but ordered me withal to set down in writing a full account thereof, expressing the most material circumstances of the whole design, which might prove serviceable for a right information of others; it so happened that the report of this royal commission, being extended far and near, gave birth to a world of tedious and importunate queries, how our matters were not carried on: therefore I found

myself under a necessity of drawing up and publishing a short abstract of what, with all submission, had been presented to his said Prussian majesty and electoral highness of Brandenburgh; annexing withal such things as since that time have happened, and do now readily occur to my memory: the knowledge whereof may prove useful both to the public, and also to particular persons, as conducing to the advancement of the glory of our great GOD: reserving yet some things which may not concern every reader to know.

II. Notwithstanding the desired success of the commission aforesaid, graciously appointed for this purpose by our sovereign, many groundless reports and false surmises, nay, manifest untruths and slanders about this undertaking have hitherto been raised, whereby the whole affair has been not a little obstructed. This I think is a sufficient warrant for any one, to expose to the view of all men the truth in its native simplicity; especially by such an historical account, in order both to vindicate his own innocence, and to ward off the open assaults of malignant tongues. These considerations then have moved me to set down a free and impartial account of this affair, which no body ought to look on as a *private* concern, it being undoubtedly a work designed and set up for *public* use and benefit. No man of any discretion, or of a candid disposition, will find reason to question the truth of what has been delivered in so plain a narrative; it being grounded partly on the inquiry of our governors, and their fatherly care over their subjects, and partly on the evidence of the thing itself: which would give me just cause to fear that I should be convinced of the contrary, if I had made the least attempt to violate the truth. Not to mention at this time, that a man of probity and temper can never presume to cast any aspersion of falshood upon the account here given; the undertaking here described being altogether void of visible supplies, and of all certainty of human supports; and depending entirely upon the blessing of GOD; so that if he should withold the same, nothing less would ensure than a sudden declension and final overthrow of what had been so happily begun; since the using ill means to effect our design, would cause the displeasure of GOD against it, and deprive us of the influence of that divine benediction which we have hitherto enjoyed.

But what is yet more for the purpose, I add, that for the sake of these, who being prejudiced against us, do not scruple to call in question the most evident things, which are even as clear as the sun at noon day, I testify, in the presence of the living GOD, *who is ready to bring to light the hidden things of darkness, and will make manifest the counsels of the heart*, that not one false word has willingly and wittingly been uttered in this whole discourse. Now, if this asseveration will not prevail neither, there is no other way left to convince people, but that GOD himself beareth witness unto the Truth by continuing his blessing upon us, and granting success to our endeavours in this affair, till he declare in the last day, before angels and men, that which now perhaps will not be believed.

III. We may here make a reasonable application of the words of the angel Raphael in the book of Tobit: *It is good to praise* GOD, *and exalt his Name, and honorably to shew forth the Works of* GOD; *therefore be not slack to praise him. It is good to keep close the secrets of a king, but it is honorable to reveal the Works of* GOD. Tob. xii. 5, 6, 7. Now, whereas Satan hitherto, by his instruments, has diffused his virulent malice against this undertaking, and spread abroad a world of lies and calumnies, should not all this stir up a man's conscience, by a true and sincere account, to set the *Work of GOD* against the lies of the devil; that so the mouth of the latter may be stopped, and the Name of the former highly extolled and magnified by all men?

IV. Moreover we are required by the *royal law* of love, to admonish our neighbour, if we see him sin against GOD, or to give him a seasonable caution, when he is in danger of betraying himself into error. And whereas many have already violated their consciences, by passing a rash censure upon the management of this affair, especially they whose judgments have been biassed by a multitude of false and groundless reports, which may give us just cause to fear, that the impetuous course of such slanders, raised by ill meaning people, might perhaps plunge them deeper into the guilt of wilful and uncharitable reflections; it is hoped, this large account may prove useful to prevent the bad consequences of such ill practices in time to come. Now, whoever has been prejudiced against us, may easily rectify his judgment by reading over this small Treatise.

But if he doth not think this worth his while, let him cease from speaking and thinking amiss of our enterprises: or let him know, that if he persist therein, he must expect to be called to an account by GOD, the righteous Judge, for these his uncharitable proceedings.

V. And further, it is our duty *to consider one another to provoke unto love and good works*, Heb. x. 24. Wherefore being well assured that many persons have been already excited by the report of this work, more industriously to provide for the poor and afflicted, it gives us a better ground to hope, that this full Narrative, laying open to every man's view the whole scope of the undertaking, will produce a still happier effect, and revive in many souls a true sense of Christian charity, wheresoever and to whomsoever it comes: which may the more rationally be expected, after the confutation of such false and slanderous reports as hitherto have cast an *odium* upon this affair, and the subsequent declaration of the truth freely presented to the reader.

VI. When, about three or four years ago, but a short account of the rise and progress of our undertaking, so far as it was then advanced under the blessing of GOD, was drawn up and presented to the public, it did not produce any ill, but rather good effects in the minds of such as read it, and proved an occasion of extolling the Name of the LORD in many places; so that several editions of the *historical account*, then published, were sold off in a little time, and the continuation thereof most earnestly desired. But since this work is considerably increased, and many remarkable instances of the wonderful Providence of GOD declared, so that the former narrative is upon no account to be compared with this, we may from thence reasonably infer, that this will still produce more noble effects, and illustrate the goodness of GOD in a more conspicuous manner.

VII. To instance in one particular. I can assure the reader, that many souls laboring both under penury of *worldly estate*, and want of *confidence* in GOD, have mightily been supported and strengthened by this his signal Providence manifested in this affair: nay, even upon the hearing of some one instance wherein the LORD hath been a present help in the day of necessity and trouble. And though they, who depending upon the abundance of their riches, and have but little regard to their duty of depending upon GOD, shall be called to an account for the haughty and scornful construction they perhaps will put upon this narrative; yet I am sure that those who are assaulted with temptations to diffidence, or lie under poverty and other distress, will be thankful to GOD for so many evident demonstrations, that GOD is still the same he hath been in times of old, and never leaves them in confusion that cast their care upon him, and learn with patience to wait for the appointed time of his gracious visitation.

VIII. The *Works of GOD* have commonly the greatest influence upon future ages: on the contrary, they in whose time they were done, too commonly undervalue them, and harden themselves against them, by permiting themselves to be overswayed by the damning sin of unbelief. Therefore it is hoped that GOD, according to his infinite mercy and goodness, will hand down this present Narrative for a memorial to after-ages, that they may magnify His Name, and acknowledge that he only is the LORD Almighty, and there is none like him.

These are the real motives which have induced me to the publication of this present account. if any one should offer to brand me with the imputation of some other design, and charge me with ambition, vain glory, self-interest, or any other aspersions of that nature, I will leave him to GOD and his own conscience. I will add but one thing: *Judge nothing before the time, until the* LORD *come; at whose coming every man's work shall be made manifest: for the day shall declare it.* The LORD direct all our endeavours to his own honor, and the benefit of our fellow creatures: which is the hearty wish of the Author.

CHAP I.

Of the Rise, Occasion, and Progress of this Undertaking.

I. As for the rise, occasion, and progress of the whole affair, some account thereof has been communicated to the public some years since, which I shall here summarily repeat, and afterwards bring down the narrative to the present time.

It is a custom of long standing, as well in the city as the suburbs of Hall, to appoint a particular day every week, wherein the poor are ordered to appear together, at the doors of such charitable persons as are disposed to bestow their benevolence upon them. Now Thursday being set apart for this purpose in my neighbourhood, (being minister at Glaucha) upon this occasion the poor flocked together before my door, and I caused some bread to be distributed among them. Whereupon it readily came into my mind, how happy an opportunity this might prove, to provide for them also some wholesome directions out of the Word of GOD; more nearly concerning them than any outward food, as tending to promote the welfare of their souls: this sort of people lying generally under gross ignorance; whence being void of all sense of religion, they betake themselves to an evil and dissolute course of life.

One day, as they gave attendance at my door, in expectation of some temporal supply, I got them all together into the house, and placed the adult persons on one side, and the youth on the other; and then familiarly and obligingly enquired of the latter, what they understood of the principles of Christian Religion, as they are set down in Luther's Catechism? The elder persons only attended to my discourse with the younger: and after I had spent about a quarter of an hour in this catechetical exercise, I concluded with a prayer: and then, according to custom, distributed my alms among them; telling them withal, that now for the future both spiritual and temporal provision was designed for them, and exhorting them to meet every Thursday on that account in my house, which they did accordingly. This exercise was begun about the beginning of the year 1694.

II. Being thus engaged with the poor, and by that means perceiving their ignorance and want of instruction to be so great, that I scarce knew where to begin the cultivation of so barren a soil, in order to plan therein a right apprehension of Christian principles; I was then heartily concerned to contrive a method for removing obstructions, and making way for better impressions on their ignorant minds; being full convinced that such defects in matter of religion, and of a religious conduct, whereby so many people debase their nature even to brutality, and abandon themselves to the government of sensuality, must needs prove a visible overthrow as well of religion as of the commonwealth. And I was made yet more sensible of this, by observing that so many children, which by reason of their parents poverty are never put to school, and so never get the least tincture of good education, remain under the grossest ignorance; whereby licentiousness and irreligion get the ascendant over them; and so being fit for no honest employment, they will not scruple in process of time to commit theft, robbery, and other such heinous crimes, which make the objects of their study and practice.

Having determined to put children to school, defraying the weekly charges thereof, I observed that they were punctual enough in fetching the money; but either did not frequent the school at all, or when they did, yet gave not the least sign of improvement in their behaviour.

III. Besides this, I was much concerned for poor housekeepers, who forbear to seek relief by begging abroad. To support whom in some measure, I bought an *alms-box*; and this I caused to be handed about every week to well-disposed students, and all such as were willing to contribute to so good a work. And by this method, in a week's time I raised about two shillings, which I applied to the relief of the aforesaid indigent housekeepers.

IV. But after we had continued to follow this practice a little while, the box seemed to prove a burden to some, and I collected so little, that it would not countervail the pains taken about it; therefore it was offered to none but those that were readily predisposed to acts of charity. But most of these were, for want of money, incapable of promoting the design: and as for the richer sort, we were not willing to run the risk of exposing our box to them; fearing they should refuse to part with the smallest limb of their golden idol; they having never had any true experience of a self-denying and mortified course of life; though some of them now and then might make indeed a plausible shew of religious duties, and pretend to pass for good Christians.

V. So I laid this quite aside, and fixed a box in my own parlour, with these words written over it; *Whoso hath this world's good, and seeth his brother have need, and shutteth up his bowels of compassion from him, how dwelleth the love of* GOD *in him?* 1 John iii. 17. And under it: *Every man according as he purposeth in his heart, so let him give; not grudgingly, or of necessity: for* GOD *loveth a cheerful giver.* 2 Cor. ix. 7. This was intended for a tacit admonition to all that came in, to open their hearts towards the poor. The box was put up in the beginning of the year 1695.

VI. And thus I was taken up a great while, with contriving effectual methods to provide for the poor, and each of them hath been blessed in its degree.

One day before I fixed the aforesaid box for the poor in my house, I took the Bible, and, as it were by accident, did light on these words: GOD *is able to make all grace abound towards you, that ye always having all sufficiency in all things, may abound to every good work.* 2 Cor. ix. 8. This sentence made a deep impression on my mind, causing me to think, "How is GOD able to make this? I should be glad to help the poor, had I wherewithal; whereas now I am forced to send many away empty and unrelieved." Some hours after I received a letter from a friend, who heavily complained that he and all his family were like to perish with want; saying, he would borrow no more; but if any one would, for GOD's sake, make him an object of his charity, he should ever retain a grateful remembrance of it. This minded me afresh of what I had read a little while before, and made still a deeper impression on me, attended with sighs and aspirations. After some debates in my mind, I thought on a project how to relieve effectually this poor man in his present want, and yet in a Christian manner, and without giving the least trouble to any person whatsoever. This then I speedily put in execution, and the said family was so successful as to get, within the compass of one year, about an hundred and fifty crowns by this means: and so their falling into extreme poverty was happily prevented. This proved a sufficient demonstration how GOD is able to make us abound to every good work: which I could not forbear here to mention, because it helps to discover as well the outward cause which our undertaking took its rise from, as the frame of my mind, which the LORD upheld for carrying on the work.

VII. About a quarter of a year after the box was set up in my house, a certain person put into it, at one time, to the value of *eighteen shillings and sixpence*, English. When I took this into my hands, I said, in full assurance of faith, "This is now a considerable fund, worthy to be laid out in some important undertaking; therefore I will even take this for the foundation of a charity-school." I did not confer with flesh and blood about this affair, but went on with resolution: and the very same day caused as many books to be bought as cost eight shillings; and then got a poor student to teach the children two hours in a day, promising him twelve pence[7] a week for his pains; in hopes the LORD would increase our small stock, after about two crowns should be thus spent in the space of eight weeks. The poor young vagrants that we had, readily accepted of these new

---

[7] It is to be observed here, that one English penny being reduced to German coin, will answer the value of sixpence in Germany, so that twelve pence English will go as far in that country as six shillings here. Which I once for all have observed in this place, lest any one being unacquainted with the customs of Germany, compute their money by the English standard, and so charge the author with stinginess in the management of his expences.

books that were offered to them; but of twenty-seven books that were distributed amongst them, four only came to our hands again, the rest being kept or sold by the children, who went away with them, and never came near us any more.

I was not discouraged by this disappointment, but having bought more books with half a crown that was left of our stock, I ordered the children to leave them behind when they had learned their lesson. Afterwards we had a press made on purpose, out of which they took their books when they came to school, and when they went away their books were locked up again: which ever since hath been the constant custom in all charity-schools.

VIII. About Easter 1695, this charity-school was begun with the above-mentioned small provision. This *eighteen shillings and sixpence* proved not only the first foundation and fund the charity-schools were grounded upon, but within the space of a little time, occasioned and produced the building of the Hospital itself!

For the charity-school, I got a place fitted up before my study, and caused a box to be fixed on one of the walls, at the top whereof I placed these words: "For defraying the charges of putting to school poor children, and providing books and other necessaries for them. Anno MDCXCV." At the bottom I set down the words of Solomon: *He that hath pity upon the poor, lendeth unto the* LORD: *and that which he hath given, will he pay him again.* Prov. xix. 17.

About Whitsuntide some friends came to pay me a visit, and seeing our endeavours, were so much affected therewith, that they readily contributed some crowns for carrying on the work. And so from time to time something was put in for forwarding the design.

IX. After Whitsuntide, some of the citizens seeing that particular care was taken for teaching the poor children, grew desirous to send their own children to the same master, and offered him weekly *two pence* each. This obliged the master to teach five hours a day, who had now weekly for his pains *two shillings and sixpence*. Amongst the poor some alms were distributed twice or thrice a week, both to render them the more willing to come to school, and to keep them the better in awe.

When this little beginning came to be known abroad, several persons sent money to support the undertaking, and others, parcels of linen to shift the children withal; to prepare their minds, by such seasonable benefits, for an earlier reception of those good directions as were to be given them.

This was the condition wherein our charity-school was in the summer time. The number of the poor and citizens children that were taught, increased to fifty, or sixty. In the mean time the blessing of GOD attending these small beginnings was so plentiful, that we were able not only to push on the most principal design, but to relieve also in some measure the poor housekeepers; there being never any settled provision, but as GOD gave it, so it was spent.— *Freely we received, and we freely gave.*

X. The summer, 1695, I received a letter from a well-disposed person of quality, wherein five hundred crowns[8] were freely offered me, to be distributed amongst the poor, according as I should think fit; provided that I should remember poor students, and let them have a share in it. Some time after the five hundred crowns were paid down; and I was not a little affected with the providential blessing, attending in so eminent a manner our endeavours; and found myself greatly encouraged to carry on the design so happily begun, because I saw the benediction of the LORD now grow more conspicuous; for as much as hitherto we had had but a few single crowns to be laid out on this account. Now this remarkable relief being delivered to me, with an order that in disposal thereof I should take care of some poor students, I presently got together such of them as seemed to be most necessitous, and best worthy of such a charitable provision, and gave them according to the condition I found them severally in. I gave to some *eight pence,* to others *sixteen pence,* and to some *two shillings* a week; so that by this means, many a student, who by reason of his poverty could not have subsisted in the university any longer, was freely maintained.

---

[8] One hundred pounds sterling, English.

The number of these poor scholars quickly increased to upwards of twenty. And this was the first occasion that moved me to admit poor students to partake of the benefit of the hospital, which has been continued to this very day. For at that time the spring of the LORD began to open itself towards indigent scholars, and its emanations have been never yet exhausted. Praised be the Name of the LORD.

XI. This soon was followed by the liberality of another person of quality, who in the same summer sent an hundred crowns[9] to be laid out for the maintenance of our poor; and a well-disposed friend sent likewise twenty crowns towards upholding the charity-school. So that GOD mightily supported what was begun, and his bounty streamed down more and more plentifully, to shew us he was ready to do still greater things, if we could but believe.

XII. About harvest I was to provide a room for the charity-school: and there being no conveniency in the parsonage-house, I hired a room in the next house. But the number of citizens and of poor people's children increased to that degree, that I found myself under a necessity to hire one room more at the beginning of the winter. And thereupon I divided the children, and appointed a particular master to instruct the citizens children, and another

---

[9] Twenty pounds, English.

to manage the poor children. Each of these masters taught four hours a day, and had half a crown each allowed them weekly, besides lodging and firing.

XIII. But now I saw how all our endeavours, even upon those very children which seemed the most hopeful, were very much frustrated; because the good impressions, which perhaps during their stay in the school were stamped on their mind, were obliterated again whilst they were abroad: and so the intended rectification of their ill habits was much obstructed. This made me resolved to single out some children, and the venture upon their maintenance and their education too. And this was the first occasion that prepared my mind to concert measures for setting up an Hospital, even before I knew of any fund whereon to raise my design.

When I came to discover this project to some well-meaning friends, I presently found one well-disposed person, who freely inclined to contribute five hundred crowns in order to facilitate this business; the interest whereof, *viz.* twenty-five crowns, he ordered yearly to be paid about Christmas, which has been done duly ever since. When I saw this blessing of GOD, I looked out for some one fatherless child to be trained up by this yearly revenue. But so it happened, that four fatherless and motherless sisters were presented to me; from amongst whom I was to choose one.

I ventured, in the Name of GOD, to take them all four; but one of them being provided for by others,

I took the remaining three, and the place of the fourth was presently supplied by another. These four I put out to persons that had a good sense of religion, to be educated by them; allowing two shillings a week for each of them.

But now that happened to me, which is usual to persons under such circumstances as mine were; I mean, if one hath but courage enough to bestow one groat upon the poor, he afterwards will be as willing to part with a crown. Having thus made a beginning, in the Name of GOD, to take effectual care of some poor, without any settled provision, and without any regard to human supports, I relied entirely upon Him, and so did not scruple to make daily addition to the number of our children.

XIV. Thus the first foundation of our hospital was laid; not upon any settled fund gathered in before hand for this purpose, neither upon any sure promise of great persons, as if they had engaged their word to defray the costs, and supply us with every thing necessary for carrying on this affair, as hath been since reported by some, and conjectured by others; it being entirely grounded upon the Providence of our great GOD.—"And he *that begins in* GOD, *will surely be able to finish.*"

XV. The next day after I had provided for the aforesaid four fatherless children, two more came in; and the day after that, another; two days after this, one more; and a week after, another was taken in: and so about the 16th of November, the number amounted to *nine*, which were committed to the care of several persons of known integrity. For these I appointed a student of divinity, whose name was George Henry Newbawer, to be their overseer or inspector, who was instructed with all things necessary for their maintenance; an account whereof he afterwards delivered to me; and took care they should want nothing material for a good education. And thus we had poor children brought together, even before we had built or bought an house for them.

XVI. In the mean time I found myself effectually supported by his hand who is the true Father of the fatherless, and *who is able to do exceeding abundantly abode all that we ask or think*, and this even beyond the expectation and dictates of my own foolish and scrupulous reason. For he inclined the heart of the same person of quality, who had contributed in ready money the before-mentioned five hundred crowns, to make a generous addition to it, and lay out the sum of a thousand crowns[10] more for the same use. In the midst of the winter, another person of eminent degree was moved to supply us with three hundred crowns,[11] to promote the education of the poor. Another person sent also a hundred crowns. Not to mention other small sums which fell in at several times.—*O that men would praise the* LORD

---

[10] Two hundred pounds sterling.

[11] Sixty pounds.

for his goodness, and for his wonderful works to the children of men.

Being thus supplied and sustained by the mercy of GOD, we were not only enabled to lend an helping hand to many poor students; to defray the charge of maintaining the orphans; to provide them with linen and cloth, and to keep up our charity-school in a flourishing state; but now an house was purchased, and about the spring also a back house added. For as the undertaking first was begun in Faith, so it was now to be advanced in the same singleness of mind, and entire dependence on GOD, without entering into disputes, *pro* and *con*, with the nice suggestions of human reason; which foreseeing a future want, is too apt to fly back and break even the best ordered and concerted measures: therefore laying aside all such suspicious apprehensions, we begun to lay a firm foundation for an Hospital. However, we took care not to mispend so much as a farthing; but to provide only such things as were absolutely necessary for the maintenance of the poor:—"knowing that Faith works boldly, when she is employed about real necessaries."

XVII. Now as soon as the back house was put in pretty good repair, and partly by mending the old rooms, partly by addition of some new ones, fitted up for the reception of the poor children, I removed the twelve orphans (for so many we had now got together) from the persons hitherto intrusted with their care, and lodged them in this house, where the before-mentioned student, who was their overseer, undertook the management of them, and furnished them with diet, cloaths, bedding, and other necessaries; trained them up in cleanliness, provided them with good schooling, and kept them in good order and discipline; and so, under GOD, proved a father to them. This was begun in the year 1696, a week before Whitsuntide.

XVIII. Under this kind of management the children were about seven weeks; and the LORD graciously relieving our wants, so favored the design, that by little and little, a larger project was set on foot, to bring the hospital to a firmer and more compleat settlement. So we got together not only all necessary utensils and furniture, especially a great many bedsteads and feather beds, (because we thought there was sufficient reason to lay every child by himself) but there was also a well and a cellar dug, and both of them were finished by the time of harvest 1696. And now the number of our children being increased to eighteen, I found myself obliged to appoint a distinct person to look after their diet; the whole proving too heavy a task for one man.

XIX. In the mean time, I ordered the poor students to come every week, at a set time, to fetch their allowance. And a particular care was taken to regulate their manners and studies, and to influence them with a regard to the honor of GOD in prosecuting the same; and so to spend the benefit bestowed on them, answerably to the design proposed therein. However, I met with such difficulties in bringing them to an apprehension thereof, that I thought myself unable to prevent their mispending some of the money, especially in such a company of young and extravagant persons. This then made me resolve, in the Name of GOD, freely to board all these students, instead of the ready money, hitherto distributed amongst them, that so I might perfectly cure the aforesaid disorders. So I cast myself upon the Providence of the LORD, hoping that his bounty, from time to time, would supply us with such relief as was sufficient for them.

This manner of proceeding taught me, 1. That this way of managing poor students proved more beneficial for them, though it was more expensive than the former. 2. How fair an opportunity this might be, to discover more and more the temper and disposition of each of them, and so to keep under stricter awe the whole tenor of their conversation. 3. How it might prove a means to detect any among them who perhaps were not under such necessity as they gave out: for these would now rather withdraw from such mean provision, and look for more dainty fare to gratify their sensuality.

It was the 13th of September, 1696, when two such tables for poor students were set up. For regulation of their manners at table, several orders were compiled, to prevent all sorts of disorders and indecencies.

Out of the number of these students the masters were chosen for the charity-school, and care taken that every thing might be done with mutual concurrence.

XX. The number of the classes being now increased, and the tables of the students set up, one house would not serve our turn, and I was compelled to look out for more room, and so to hire another house, which was the very next to our hospital: and in this I lodged the steward; the two yards being brought into one. Sometime after I bought this house for three hundred crowns.[12]

XXI. As the first beginning for laying a foundation of this work, was occasioned by the poor that begged at the door, so afterwards an especial care was constantly taken, not only for this sort of children, but also for people broken with old age and poverty. And as heretofore Thursday was fixed for distributing alms amongst them, so afterwards Tuesday was added, wherein they are catechised, and when that is over, they receive the charity.

XXII. No less care has been taken for the better regulation of the charity-school. At first it was divided into two classes; one appointed for poor boys, and the other for poor girls: but when these came to be overstocked, new distinctions were

---

[12] Sixty pounds sterling.

contrived, according to the age and stature of the children; so that the whole is now divided into four forms, or classes; that is, one for the *bigger*, and one for the *lesser* boys: and so likewise for the girls. These four classes have hitherto been constantly maintained; each of them having a particular master assigned, with a room fit for their purpose, and books necessary. So that the whole crowd of beggarly children dispersed all about the town, and as many as are in no condition to pay for their schooling, may freely enjoy here the benefit of being taught gratis.

XXIII. Those schools have been likewise promoted, which were set up at the request of the citizens, for their children. And another was set up in the month of September, 1697, for such of the citizens boys as were to be instructed in the fundamental points of learning. But in the year 1699, on the 18th of May, this school was united with that class of the poor children which are taught languages and sciences: whereupon they were divided into three classes in all ,as well to keep them more easily in order, as to manage them the better, according to the different degrees of their proficiency; each of them being governed by distinct matters, who are to teach them both Latin, Greek and Hebrew; with history, geography, geometry, music, and botany.

There have in like manner been school-masters appointed in other places, for such children as were either wholly excluded the benefit of the public schools by reason of the remote distance of their parents, or else came but very seldom, and that too at unseasonable hours.

As for the maintenance of the schools for citizens children, their parents contribute something to support them; but that not sufficing for the full maintenance thereof, I have been necessitated to supply the rest, out of that stock Divine Providence hitherto hath provided for the poor and charity-schools, that so I might prevent their coming to nothing.

XXIV. It was found necessary to appoint two masters for the fatherless children; one for the boys, and one for the girls: and if any amongst the boys were observed to be of good natural parts, and quick apprehension, such were singled out from amongst the rest, and provided with particular masters, to instruct them not only in writing and arithmetic, but also in languages and sciences, as was mentioned before: and this practice has been continued to this present time. The rest of the boys which are to be bred to handycraft trades, are put into two ranks, and taught by several masters.

XXV. After some time, the number as well of the poor children, as of the students, increasing, and the small house which was at first provided for them, proving now too strait, I was obliged to think of procuring one that was bigger. But the setting up of hospitals being yet an uncommon thing in this country, I resolved to make some enquiry into the nature of such as had been erected in other parts; and because the accounts which either in print or manuscript came to my hands about this affair, did not satisfy me, I farther resolved to send the aforesaid George Henry Newbauer into Holland, the seat of good charity-schools and colleges of this nature; who thereupon was dispatched hence, June the 2d, in the year 1697: and his main scope was to take an exact survey of the hospitals there; of their structure, their orders, with the manner of carrying on such works; and to take particular notice of all such things as might any way be helpful to us in erecting this house of charity.

XXVI. In the mean time we did not think we should lie under any pressing necessity of making too much haste to effect this our design, because we had bought for a sum of one thousand nine hundred and fifty crowns,[13] the house called the Golden Eagle, lying without the gate called Rannish Gate, and the garden thereunto belonging: and this we designed to fit up for the reception of all our poor. But we quickly found that this house, being built for an inn, would not afford such conveniences as were requisite for an hospital.

XXVII. Besides this, we were also to consider, that others offered to build an alehouse directly opposite the said Golden Eagle; and this tending to

---

[13] Four hundred and eighty-seven pounds.

the no small disadvantage of the hospital, I found myself under a necessity to purchase that ground too; promising withal to fill up that empty space with some useful building. And further laying myself under other tedious and pressing circumstances, occasioned as well by the house I had bought, as by the several houses already hired for a pretty large rent, I was excited more and more to the following attempt.

XXVIII. As the whole affair was never undertaken upon any settled provision, but in singleness of heart, and entire dependence upon GOD Almighty; so I had not as much now as would suffice to erect a small house, much less a large and public hospital. Yet the LORD, by his infinite Mercy, supported me with such a presence of mind, (for which his Name be praised) that I immediately resolved to lay the foundation of a new building in the place that was before bought. For this purpose I recalled out of Holland the before-mentioned Newbauer. In the year 1698, July the 5th, the place being surveyed and adjusted, they began to break ground; which being finished a few days after, on the 13th of July the foundation for an Hospital was laid, in the Name of GOD. The LORD had provided so much money in readiness as enabled us to procure a good quantity of timber; but as for the building itself, I was now to wait upon GOD, and from week to week, to receive at his hand what he would be graciously pleased to furnish me with for carrying on the same:—GOD knowing that I was not fit for an independent.

XXIX. When I first went about this work, my design was indeed to set up only a timber house; and accordingly the foundation was laid several feet long, suitable to the projected building. But in the mean time the master-builder using several weighty arguments, made me change my first resolution, and to declare for a building of stone; especially after he had conferred about this affair with divers other skilful and eminent men; by whose approbation I was still more confirmed in this design.

Another inducement was, that having about Easter, in the same year, bought, for the benefit of the poor, a small farm, with an adjacent piece of ground, there was in the garden thereof a rock, which would afford such stones as were fit for raising up a wall. This proved no small advantage for facilitating the work now resolved on, especially since some well-disposed persons, who favored the undertaking, did of their own accord offer to cause these stones to be brought to the place that was marked out for the building; which was done accordingly.

Yet all these motives together had not prevailed with me to that degree, if the LORD had not (as all along, so now in these particular circumstances) strengthened and inclined me to venture it *upon his assistance*, and resolutely to conclude what was now to be done.

So the work was begun without any settled provision, and the LORD, from time to time, seconded the enterprize with such a blessing, that even the builders and workmen cheerfully went about the business by reason of their pay. And it afforded no small satisfaction of mind to many of them, that each day's work was begun with prayer; and Saturdays, when they got their weekly pay, now and then finished with good admonitions, prayers, and thanksgivings, for the assistance we had that week received at the hand of the LORD.—*He that will observe these things, even he shall understand the loving kindness of the* LORD.

The building ran up amain, and after such a rate, that in the year 1699, by the 13th of July, that is, within the space of one year, they were ready to cover it with the roof; though the nature of the ground required a very deep and strong foundation. And this was the reason that about harvest, 1698, the structure was raised but a few feet above ground.

By this forwardness of our work, the LORD actually confuted the incredulity of that man, who, when the wall was half done, most presumptuously burst out into this impious expression; "If this wall comes to be finished, I will hang myself on it."

About Easter 1700, the orphans and the students begun actually to dine in the hospital, and soon after they got lodgings in one part of the house. And at Easter 1701, the rest of the house was inhabited;

which did not a little contribute towards accomplishing the whole affair.

His Electoral Highness, to encourage these endeavours, was pleased to furnish us with one hundred thousand bricks, and thirty thousand tiles, which proved very beneficial in promoting the building. Which we cannot but mention with humble thankfulness towards his Electoral Highness:—but much more to the honor of GOD, who inclined his heart.

XXX. In the year 1698, September the 19th, his Electoral Highness of Brandenburgh was further pleased to provide the hospital with a charter, which afterwards by way of confirmation, he was pleased to explain in several points.

XXXI. After the LORD had thus provided for the orphans, and given many happy demonstrations of his fatherly Providence over them, he now farther inclined the heart of an eminent and well-disposed gentleman, to employ a part of his estate in making a *settlement for the maintenance of some poor widows*, and to intrust me with the management thereof. Accordingly in the year 1698, about the spring, an house was bought in the street called Gomer Street, at Glaucha. In the summer it was enlarged, and made fit for the reception of four widows, a maid, and a chaplain; into which one widow was admitted September 19th, 1698, and soon after three more.

XXXII. Now in this hospital for poor widows, four of them are maintained, who, besides the provision of their lodging, firing, and candles, have two shillings a week each, to maintain themselves in diet; and every year a shift, a pair of shoes, and, within the compass of two years, a new suit of cloaths, if they want it.—*Thus* GOD, *who clothes grass, and adorns the lily, will much more clothe us, O we of little faith!*

If they are able to get any thing by their labor, as by spinning, or needle-work, they may keep it for their own use. They have also a garden near the house.

XXXIII. For these aged widows there is not only appointed a chaplain, of good and pious behaviour, to go to prayer with them twice a day, but also a maid (as was hinted before) to serve them, to buy such things as are necessary for them, and to nurse them, if they happen to fall sick. The physician that is appointed over the hospital, prescribes them medicines, which are provided for them out of the common stock,—which, blessed be GOD, is not exhausted.

CHAP. II.

Of the visible and wonderful Providence of GOD, *attending these Endeavours, to establish the Hospital and Charity-Schools, from their first Rise to the present Time.*

I. It being almost impossible to have full insight into the means, whereby as well the charity-schools as the ensuing building were both begun and carried on, except there be given some instances of the wonderful Providence of the LORD, whereby he hath remarkably signalized his care and assistance in advancing this affair

I will here set down a good number of such providential occurrences as seem the most conspicuous to me.

II. By the foregoing narrative, any one may see that the design was not first to provide a settled fund, and then to go about the work: but, on the contrary, that which the LORD bestowed on us, as the means of a present support, was readily and without delay employed, though it made up but a few crowns, and our care for a future supply was by faith committed to the LORD. Likewise, that not only the charity-schools were thus begun, but the actual entertaining and maintaining of the orphans, and of the poor students; nay, the building of the house itself was in the same way begun, and carried on. From whence any understanding man may easily gather, that the management of this business must have been now and then attended with many extraordinary circumstances; it being not carried on by the usual manner of money received and laid out. Which shall now be exemplified by the following instances.

III. Before Easter 1696, I found the provision for the poor very low, and so far exhausted, that I did not know where to get any thing towards defraying the charges of the ensuing week; (which happened before I had been used to such awakening trials:) but GOD was pleased to relieve our want in a very seasonable hour, and by an unexpected help. He inclined the heart of a person, (who it was, where residing, or of what sex, the LORD knoweth) to pay down one thousand crowns for the relief of the poor: and this sum was delivered to me in such a time, when our provision was brought even to the last crumb. The LORD, whose work this was, be praised for ever, and reward this benefactor with his blessings a *thousand fold*;—for surely the LORD bestowed on that person a liberal heart.

IV. At another time all provision was gone, when the steward declared there was a necessity of buying some cattle to furnish the table, and of providing twenty or thirty bushels of flour, to be laid up;

besides other necessaries, as wood, wool, &c. if we would manage our business to the best advantage. These necessities being offered up unto GOD, as the Father of the fatherless, an opportunity was presented to discover our straits to a person who was then with us, and who in all likelihood would readily have supplied our want to the utmost of his power. But I thought it more convenient to give GOD the glory, and not to stir from before his door; He himself being able to assist us in such a way, as both his Providence might be thereby rendered the more conspicuous, and his Name more cheerfully extolled. And another reason why I was shy of adventuring upon this person, was, because the same had already shewn some tokens of his charitable inclination towards our poor.

In the midst of these pressing circumstances, I found one comfort, which was a presence of mind in prayer, joined with a confidence dependence upon that LORD *who heareth the young ravens when they cry.* When prayer was over, and I was just sitting down at the table, I heard somebody knock at the door; which when I opened, there was an acquaintance of mine holding in his hand a letter, and a parcel of money wrapt up, which he presented to me. I found therein fifty crowns, being sent a great way: and this gift was soon followed by twenty crowns more. This proved a seasonable relief, and suitably supply to our then low condition; and a proof that the LORD had heard even before we cried unto him; whereby his Name was not a little magnified.

V. In the year 1698, in the month of October, I sent a *ducat*[14] to a very poor woman, living out of this town, who, through many trials and afflictions, had obtained an entrance into a real sense of religion. This woman writ me word, "that the ducat I sent her came just at the time when she extremely wanted such an help; and that she had thereupon immediately prayed GOD to reward our poor with a great many more ducats." Soon after this, a well-meaning person offered me one single ducat and twelve double ducats: and on the same day, a friend also out of Sweedland[15] sent two ducats; which soon were followed by twenty-five others, sent by the post in a letter, from an unknown hand; the person sending them not thinking fit to express his (or her) name; and by twenty more, which were presented to our poor by an eminent patron.

About the same time Prince *Lewis* of Wurtemburg died at Eisenach, and I received an intimation that he had bequeathed a sum of money to the Hospital. It happened to be five hundred ducats[16] in gold, put up in a little bag, with this direction, "For the Hospital at Hall." These five hundred ducats were

---

[14] Nine shillings and sixpence.

[15] Sweden. (M.S.)

[16] Two hundred and sixty-eight pounds fifteen shillings.

afterwards delivered to me, according to the design of the testator, and truly at such a time when there was great occasion for them to carry on the building. Now when I saw this heap of ducats, I remembered the prayer of that pious woman who "intreated the LORD to reward our poor again with many ducats."—Thus the believing poor can help with their prayers, if they cannot with their cash.

VI. In the year 1699, about February, I found myself under great straits; and in deed it was an hour of probation. All our provision being spent, and the daily necessity of the poor calling for large supplies, I closely adhered in my mind to this saying, *Seek first the kingdom of* GOD, *and his righteousness, and all these things shall be added unto you*; avoiding temporal cares, and turning the whole bent of my soul upon a close union with GOD: and when I was now laying out the last of the money, I said in my thoughts, "LORD, look upon my necessity." Then going out of my chamber in order to repair to the college, where I was to attend my public lecture, I unexpectedly found a student in my house, that waited for my coming out, and presented me the sum of seventy crowns, that was sent by some friends, to support the necessity of the hospital, from a place above two hundred English miles distant.

Now this, though it would hardly hold out half a week, by reason of the great expences I was then obliged to defray, yet the LORD soon after sent us in a fresh supply, and within the space of a few weeks, carried me so through these trials, that neither the frame of my mind was discomposed within, nor our want discovered by any token without;—which was a great blessing; as the least shew of distrust of GOD, casts a reflection on his honor, and stumbles the weak in faith.

VII. Soon after this, there was want again in every corner. The steward brought his book, and desired me to defray the weekly charges. My recourse was to GOD, through faith. The expences were necessary, and I saw not the least provision, nor any way to procure it. This made me resolve to retire into my closet, and to beg the LORD's assistance in so pressing a necessity; but I designed first to finish the task I then was about, being employed in dictating something.

Having done with this, and preparing now for prayer, I received a letter from a merchant, intimating that he was ordered to pay a thousand crowns to me for the relief of the hospital. This put me in mind of that saying of the prophet, *It shall come to pass, that before they call, I will answer, and whiles they are yet speaking, I will hear.* Isaiah lxv. 24. Nevertheless I entered into my closet, but instead of begging and praying, as I had designed, I praised and extolled the Name of the LORD; and hope that others, who perhaps may come to read this, will do the like with me. And thus the Providence of GOD would actually teach me, not to put too great a confidence in a visible stock, or present support of men.

VIII. In the year 1699, March the 21st, I received a letter by the post, wherein were inclosed four ducats,[17] with this inscription:
"This to the poor is freely sent,
For health, which GOD to me has lent."
It came to my hands in a time of trial, and when I was in great want of money.

IX. About Michaelmas, 1699, I was in great want again. In a very fair and pleasant day I took a walk, and viewing the most glorious and magnificent fabrick of the heavens, I found myself remarkably strengthened in faith; which indeed I do not ascribe to any disposition of my own, but entirely attribute it to the gracious operations of the SPIRIT of GOD on my soul. Hereupon were suggested to my mind these, and the like thoughts: "How excellent a thing it is for any one, being deprived of all outward helps, and having nothing to depend on, but having the knowledge of the living GOD, the Creator of heaven and earth, and putting his trust in Him, to rest satisfied in the extremity of poverty!"

Now though I well knew that the very same day I wanted money, yet I found myself not cast down; and just as I came home, the steward came for money to pay the workmen (it being Saturday) employed in the building of the hospital: and accordingly addressing himself to me, he said, "Is

---

[17] Two pounds three shillings.

there any money brought in?" To which I answered, "No; but I believe in GOD." Scarce was the word out of my mouth, when I was told a student desired to speak with me, who then brought thirty crowns from a person whose name he would not discover. So I went back into the room, and asked the other, how much he wanted at present? He said, "Thirty crowns." I replied, "Here they are; but do you want any more?"—"No," says he. This confirmed us both in our reliance upon the LORD, because we plainly discerned the wonderful hand of GOD, who in that very moment that we were in necessity, did supply us, and even with the *very sum* we then wanted.— The exact sum, shewed the narrow inspection of GOD; and none being sent over, left room for Faith to work.

X. Not long after, we were likewise reduced to great straits; when it happened, that four hundred crowns were sent me by the post, accompanied with a letter from a well-meaning student, intimating that this sum had been delivered to him, to relieve our hospital. I cannot express how effectual this was to renew my dependence upon the LORD; and how visibly it convinced me, that the hour of trial is only appointed by the LORD for the strengthening of our Faith. The LORD graciously remember this benefactor!

XI. Another time all our provision was spent. Then it fell out, that in addressing myself to the LORD, I found myself deeply affected with the fourth petition of the LORD's Prayer; *Give us this day our daily bread:* and my thoughts were fixed in a more especial manner upon the words *this day*, because on the very same day we had great occasion for it. While I was yet praying, a friend of mine came before my door in a coach, and brought the sum of four hundred crowns. Then I perceived the reason why I more eminently had found such a sweet savor in that expression, *this day*, and praised the LORD, in whose disposal are all things.—Thus *the morrow takes thought for the things of itself.*

XII. In the year 1700, I was sick about seven or eight weeks before Easter. On Easter Tuesday, which was the first time I went abroad, having besought the LORD that he would be pleased to *bless my going out, and coming in*, it happened, that as I was going out, a consolatory letter was delivered to me; and when I came home, another, in which was inclosed a bill of one hundred crowns for the relief of the hospital; together with an admonition, encouraging me, in a particular manner, cheerfully to go on in the work so happily begun. This letter came from a protestant merchant, living in a place about five hundred miles distant from hence. The LORD remember this benefactor!

XIII. Another time, a well-disposed person of quality, of the female sex, was present, and saw to how great want we were just then reduced. This struck the deeper into her mind, because she had been wont to assist our poor, as far as she could; but was not able, neither then, nor at any other time, to relieve our want with any considerable gift. On the same day this person happened to discourse with another lady, who was but just come to town; and this latter mentioning that she had brought along with her *a little mite for the hospital,* viz. *fifty crowns,* the first could not forbear weeping, her joy was so great; as knowing, on one hand, the utmost straits we were then in, and seeing, on the other, the present and visible supply, coming to our relief on the very same day.

XIV. At another time, when all was spent, and I knew not whence to fetch any thing, it so fell out, that a protestant merchant, almost seven hundred and fifty English miles off, sent the sum of twenty-five crowns, and desired me not to take it ill, if he put me to the trouble of dispersing it amongst the poor.

In the same manner a certain countess hath supplied me twice with twenty-five crowns, when our provision was reduced to the lowest degree. I am sure it has often happened that we have been relieved, when our provision has been just spent; though no mortal acquainted our benefactors with the necessity under which we labored, nor how seasonable it was for them to relieve us at that instant!

XV. Another time we were brought into a very low condition, when the LORD stirred up the heart of a farmer to give me as much as he could hold in his hand, being about five crowns, in small coin.

XVI. It often has happened, that, when strangers have been with me, and I have given them some account of the wonderful Providence of GOD; for their confirmation of their faith, even in their very presence something or another has been sent for the poor: an example or two whereof I shall here subjoin.

Whilst a certain well-disposed person, who bestowed twenty crowns upon the poor, was yet talking with me, a lad came in, who brought twenty crowns in ready money, with a letter, promising the yearly continuance thereof, if the LORD would be pleased to preserve life and health. The lad would not tell the name of the person that sent him, being strictly charged to the contrary, and desired only a receipt. The person whom I at first mentioned, being undoubtedly moved by so visible a proof of GOD's Providence, sent immediately fifty crowns more. The promise given in writing by the other person, hath hitherto faithfully been performed.

XVII. Another person being in my company, and to whom I was declaring some remarkable passages of GOD's Providence; whilst we were yet talking together, there were brought in three sacks filled with linen, leather for breeches, and other stuff of that nature, to clothe the children; being sent by a gentlewoman. The said person who was then with me, was not a little strengthened in the faith by so remarkable an instance.—Blessed be GOD that there is here and there a *Dorcas* left in the world.

XVIII. In the same manner I spake once to another well-meaning friend, recounting to him some evident demonstrations of the admirable Providence of the LORD; upon which he could not forbear weeping: and whilst we were discoursing together, I received a letter, with a bill of five hundred crowns; being then just reduced to such circumstances, that, humanly speaking, I saw not the least support, nor any way to obtain a supply.

XIX. Another time I fell into the deepest poverty, and, what was more, I was urged by the importunity of most that were about me, calling for a supply to their pressing necessity. But having cast my eye upon the LORD, I answered them plainly thus: "Now ye come all to seek money of me; but I know of another Benefactor to go to;" meaning the LORD. The word scarce out of my mouth, when a friend of mine, who was then just come off a journey, put privately fourteen ducats[18] into my hand; which proved a fresh instance of the endearing Providence of the LORD.—This is enough to put Infidelity out of countenance, and make her ashamed to shew her head.

XX. So it has often happened, that persons having only heard or read some account, either of the good design of the undertaking, or of the

_____

[18] Seven pounds ten shillings and sixpence.

wonderful ways by which the LORD supported us, have presently found themselves inclined to cast something into our treasury, to facilitate the affair. For instance; a certain nobleman hearing some passages of GOD's Providence over this work, freely offered to pay down yearly the sum of twenty crowns; and he has been as good as his word. A certain merchant also being once desired to exchange some ducats presented to the poor, and being acquainted withal that they did belong to the poor orphans, he not only exchanged them, but made an addition of twenty crowns more of his own.

XXI. Likewise it fell out another time that I stood in need of a great sum of money, insomuch that an hundred crowns would not have served my turn; and yet I saw not the least appearance how I might be supplied with an hundred groats. The steward came in, and set forth the want we were in. I bid him to come again after dinner; and I resolved to put up my prayers to the LORD for his assistance. When he came again after dinner, I was still in the same want, and so appointed him again to come in the evening. In the mean time a sincere friend of mine came to see me, and with him I joined in prayers, and found myself much moved to praise and magnify the LORD for all his admirable dealings towards mankind, even from the beginning of the world; and the most remarkable instances came readily to my remembrance whilst I was praying. I was so elevated in praising and magnifying GOD, that I insisted only on that exercise of my present devotion, and found no inclination to put up many anxious petitions to be delivered out of the present necessity. At length my friend taking his leave, I accompanied him to the door, where I found the steward waiting on one side for the money he wanted, and on the other side another person, who brought an hundred and fifty crowns, sealed up in a bag, for the support of the hospital.—Thus Providence kept pace with necessity.

What more illustrious proof could I expect of GOD's holy and wonderful Providence! who graciously accepteth the prayer of the poor, and comforteth those that are cast down, when they put their trust in Him; and who is still the same gracious LORD as in the times of old, when he rendered himself glorious by his dealings with the fathers; the signal examples of whose faith are recommended to our imitation.

XXII. At another time thirty crowns were required to pay off the workmen; at which time some friends of mine were with me, one of whom had promised ten crowns, and another four, for the support of the poor; but neither of them had actually paid them in, which otherwise might have been very helpful for the defraying some charges: so I was obliged for the present to dismiss the overseer of the building, who came to fetch the money, with this comfort; "The LORD, who is faithful, will take care for us." Away he went, and found the workmen before the hospital, waiting for their pay; but by the way he unexpectedly met with one of his acquaintance, to whom he unbosomed himself, and discovered the pressing circumstances he was then in; who thereupon readily lent him fourteen crowns; and so he went to pay at least some part of the money due to the workmen: but before he had done, I received above thirty crowns from another place; whereupon I immediately sent away the aforesaid thirty crowns for the workmen, and the rest was spent in providing necessaries for the poor. And this proved a fresh visible instance of Divine Providence.

XXIII. At the end of the following week we were reduced to like straits, and I was called upon for money to recruit our provision, according to custom, on Friday, and to pay the workmen on Saturday; but there was not a farthing for either of these uses. So I said, "It is now time again to rejoice; for the LORD will undoubtedly give us another instance of his Providence." I dispatched the steward with that saying of Samuel, עד תבה *Hitherto hath the* LORD *helped us.*[19] 1 Sam. vii. 12. For this expression is as it were turned into a most comfortable proverb amongst us, and experience

---

[19] The 1787 edition has the Hebrew incorrect. The intended phrase is עד הנה *'aḏ hēnnâ*, Hebrew for "hitherto." (M.S.)

hath been the most useful comment upon it. Betimes the next morning fifty crowns were sent in; by means whereof the LORD graciously carried us through the difficulties of that week.

XXIV. Another time, being reduced to the lowest ebb, and the burden of unavoidable expences lying upon the steward, he found himself oppressed with care and concern how to extricate himself. Whereupon he got together as much as he could to discharge the debts, and, amongst the rest, he sold a silver spoon that had been presented to the hospital. But all this would not serve his turn. In this extremity, an hundred crowns were delivered to me for the poor; and being thus provided, I sent presently sixty of them to the steward, and the remainder was laid out for other purposes. A few hours after I had received the above-mentioned sum, there came a letter of advice, importing that *thirteen tuns and an half of herrings* were in the way towards us, which some charitable friends had purchased for the relief of our poor; as the year before we had three tuns bestowed on us. How effectual this was to raise the languishing faith of the steward, and to refresh his mind after so many toils and cares, may, I think, be easily conjectured. He said indeed, "Now I will rejoice even in time of want, in hopes of seeing some discovery of the admirable Providence of GOD!" which had been hitherto, as he said, beyond his strength. He added likewise, that no oppressing care had ever since seized upon his mind in the midst of want and distress, but had rather rejoiced and kept up his spirit, whilst he reasoned thus with himself: "Now will I patiently wait for the wonderful help of the LORD, and see by what way or means he will be pleased to relieve our necessities.

XXV. A little while after we had another hour of probation; but the LORD was pleased to supply us then likewise with fifty crowns, which was an help not in the least foreseen: and at the same time I was acquainted that twenty-eight Cumin cheeses were forthwith to be sent from Leyden in Holland.

XXVI. Now and then it happened, that some strangers coming in to see the hospital, have put half a crown, or one or more ducats, in the box for the poor, just when we were under great difficulties; they themselves not knowing what a seasonable relief it was to us.

XXVII. Another time I was called upon, early in the morning, for some money to defray the charges of that day. I had then but six crowns left, which I readily delivered. The steward taking it into his hand, told it, and said, "If it was multiplied by six, which would make up the sum of six and thirty, it would be serve my turn." I comforted him with our manifold experience of the Divine benediction we hitherto had enjoyed; and it happened that the same GOD *multiplied* it on that very day just to the sum of thirty-six crowns, which was wanting: and this proved no small encouragement to our dependence upon GOD. Soon after it was followed by twenty-five ducats[20] more, to bear the charges of the next day. —Here Faith prescribed to GOD, and he submitted to it, with an addition.

XXVIII. Another time, being taken up with some other affairs, I quite forgot the want we did then lie under. Having thus composed my mind to a quiet frame, that I might the better dispatch my business, I received a letter, with a piece of gold, of eighteen crowns value; whereby both our want was relieved, and I myself kept free from any disturbance in my other affairs. I remembered than the saying of the LORD; *All these things shall be added unto you.*

XXIX. Upon another time, when all provision was spent, one of my fellow-laborers in the evening conference mentioned the present want, which proved a matter of comfort, and presented to us an occasion to strengthen our faith, by means of a grateful remembrance of all the benefits we had before received at the hand of GOD, and to rejoice in that particular privilege which he hath left upon sacred record, *viz.* that we need not to be careful for any thing, or disturb ourselves with perplexing thoughts, but commit all things to the gracious conduct of Divine Providence. The result of this consideration, was an hearty sense of the eminent advantage enjoyed by them that trust in GOD, whose rejoicing in the midst of poverty, is much

---

[20] Thirteen pounds eight shillings and nine pence.

more desireable, than the tormenting thoughtfulness of those, whose heart is continually oppressed with the uneasy cares of this world, attended with fearful doubts, and wavering hopes. Hereupon we put up our petitions, unanimously extolling the Name of the LORD for his infinite goodness and mercy, and resigned our present state to his fatherly protection. That very hour the LORD was pleased to incline the heart of a great man, who hitherto had favored our endeavors, to relieve our want the next morning; giving a particular charge to some of his attendants to remember him of it. Accordingly the next day he sent three hundred crowns. Upon which occasion I think fit to take notice, that a particular juncture of circumstances, working both from within and without, was observable in this affair, which rendered the Providence of GOD more conspicuous at this time.—*Who ever trusted in* GOD, *and was confounded?*

XXX. Once I remember, when all was spent, it happened, that a piece of gold, worth ten ducats, was delivered to me, for a certain godly minister, then reduced to the utmost want and poverty; and being absent, I was to send it to him. This made a joyful diversion to my mind, and made me forget the want we were then in at home. But soon after the LORD remembered also our poor; for a *gold chain*, weighing about four ounces and a half, was sent from abroad, and proved an unexpected help in our present want.

XXXI. I must needs here mention, that the Providence of GOD, in the whole undertaking, hath been the more illustriously visible, in regard of a train of many particular circumstances, and especially his inclining all manner of people to a hearty concurrence in supporting the work, after it was once begun; nay, even those from whom, being themselves under strait circumstances, no such thing was expected. To such charitable persons we may apply St. Paul's expression, 2 *Cor.* viii. 2, 3. wherein he commendeth the charitable inclinations of the Macedonians; *that in a great trial of affliction, the abundance of their joy, and their deep poverty, abounded unto the riches of their liberality. For to their power, yea, and beyond their power, they were willing of themselves.*

Some who were not able to contribute towards our support with ready money, endeavored to supply that defect by other acts of charity. Country people have caused pewter cups to be made at their own charge, and conveyed to us for the use of the hospital: and several pewterers have done the like. Others have bought pewter dishes, and plates; others, vessels of copper, for the same end. Several country women have readily bestowed some flax, and thread; others have willingly made it into linen; and others employed themselves to make shirts of it, for the use of the poor. Others have bought hats for the boys, and sent skins to make them breeches. Others have sent caps for the girls, and other things of that nature, to clothe them withal.—Thus GOD, who clothed our first parents, doth not forget their children.

Now and then it has fallen out, that well-wishers to the hospital have dressed some children from head to foot.

About Christmas and new-year's tide, and especially at the time of public examination, some have made provision for entertaining the children with a better dinner than ordinary.—Thus GOD gave them a little banqueting.

The same thing has happened in respect of diet. For some well-disposed persons, after reaping, would send in some of their corn, pease, and the like, for the poor. Others would send meat, fish, cheese, and other supplies.

Again, others who had by legacy got a parcel of books, instead of selling the same, have made them over to the hospital, which proved the foundation of erecting a library for the use of our poor students employed in the hospital.—Faith will not only bring *cloaks* to clothe the poor, *but likewise the books and the parchments.*

Others have bestowed part of the money which was left them by their deceased friends. A well-meaning friend has bestowed part of a silver mine upon us, near Kehrbach, called the New Blessing of GOD, and registered it for the Hospital at Glaucha without Hall; and he himself has undertaken the management of it, till it may advance some profit to the poor. Others have sent some of their beer when they have brewed, or some money, if they had good success therein. Others have provided some salt for the hospital; others have presented it with feather beds; others, with sheets, table cloth, &c.—This shews that not only the corn and wine, but also the *wool* and the *flax* are the LORD's.

Several merchants have sent whole pieces, or some remnants of cloth, and of stuff, as a help towards covering the bodies of the poor. Many have thought their rich dress and apparel, which served them heretofore to make a figure in the world, better bestowed, when laid out to clothe the poor. Some would turn whole suits of finery into money, sell their silver and gold laces, and clothe the poor therewith. Some have sent hither, and others have sold, silver spoons, silver buttons, silver cups, gold rings set with stones, golden bracelets, and necklaces of gold, to support the poor withal. And such things have commonly fallen out, when great want and necessity have excited us to pray for relief.—Surely this must be very offensive to the god of this world.

XXXII. What has been said hitherto, may give to the reader a pretty good apprehension under what circumstances both the education of the poor, and the erecting of the hospital, has been begun and carried on.

In the month of September, 1698, his Electoral Highness of Brandenburgh was graciously pleased to confer upon the hospital several privileges; which made some people think, that the whole concern has been ever since endowed with a fixed maintenance, and that the undertakers, after so many boisterous agitations, are happily arrived to shore.

But to lay open the matter as it is, I must needs say, that the Hand of GOD, in obtaining these privileges, was so fully discovered to me, that many presumptuous censures that have been passed upon me, have not in the least disturbed me. I am sensible of the benefits that have been derived from thence to the poor, and shall ever keep a thankful remembrance thereof both towards GOD and towards men.

But to rectify the judgments of such as have been mistaken in this affair, they ought to be acquainted, that the aforesaid privileges never had such an extensive influence upon the work, as to set it altogether upon another footing; nor have they been immediately rendered effectual. For some of them have not been as yet practicable; and others have required greater expences, as the setting up of the apothecaries and booksellers shops.——O the diligence of the devil, and his family, to rob GOD of his honor!

The chief branch of these privileges, seemed to be the *collection*, which his Electoral Highness allowed throughout the whole extent of his dominions and provinces. Now though I do not undervalue such a benefit, (it being of that nature, that not the least constrain is used upon any body, but every one is at liberty to give what he pleaseth towards the relief of the poor) yet I could not light presently on such persons as were qualified for gathering in this collection; and though at last I pitched on some who seemed to be fit for this business, yet it has hitherto met with such obstructions, that besides in Berlin, it has been yet begun but in three provinces. From whence an impartial judge may easily infer, that such a collection may give some ease to the undertaking, but can never prove a sufficient stock for the maintenance of about two hundred persons, who are to be provided for.

In the mean time, there has been spent more within half a year, than the whole collection amounted to; and to do right to the matter, what has been raised this way, only proved some help for defraying part of the charges of maintaining, cloathing, and teaching the poor.—Faith's undertakings go on best upon the LORD's *wheels*.

In short, for as much as no small time will be required before, on one side, the unjust odium the undertaking upon this account is charged with, is awarded; and on the other, the imparted privileges come to be put in practice, as they are like to prove more beneficial to the ensuing age, than I find them at present: and this, I must confess, was the main scope I had in view, when I petitioned his Electoral Highness for the grant of them. Not to mention now, that since the time these privileges have been granted, the whole affair has been not a little enlarged; by which means it has become more chargeable. All which shews the mistake of those, who, by groundless reports, have been inclined to believe, that faith and dependence upon the LORD was not any longer exercised in this business, as it was at first, but that the secular power, with a fixed allowance of provisions, did now bear the sway. This mistaken report has misled many into slanders and uncharitable censures; and others have attempted to force into the hospital all manner of poor people, upon the false supposal of rich endowments, without having made the least enquiry, whether the hospital was in a condition to relieve them or no.—So anxious is flesh and blood to exalt itself at the expence of GOD's honor.

Others have put so large a construction upon the privileges, that by their report, people in very distant places have been prevailed with to believe that twelve thousand crowns were allowed *per annum* for the maintenance of the hospital. And this has farther inclined many needy persons to come a great way off, supposing to find here a present relief both as for food and raiment, and to wonder, when the event did not answer their mistaken expectation.

And this I hope may sufficiently inform any impartial reader, that as the work hath been begun in faith and reliance upon GOD, and not in any trust upon a set stock of provisions; so it is still carried on in the same way, and under the like difficulties;

notwithstanding the small supplies coming in now and then; having as yet no other foundation than it has stood upon ever from the beginning.

XXXIII. Another branch of signal Providence over us, hath been manifested in such as fell sick. In the very beginning of our endeavors, the LORD inclined the heart of one of the chief apothecaries and chymists at Leipsick, to dispose gratis of so much physic as there was necessary for our diseased; and this he freely continued, till his Electoral Highness of Brandenburgh was graciously pleased to permit the keeping an apothecary's shop for the hospital; whereby we have been enabled to make a shift, without being any further chargeable to that worthy benefactor, who, out of his great charity, bore no small part of the burden, which usually adheres to an undertaking of this nature.

XXXIV. Another benefit which the LORD provided for us, was, that he inclined an eminent physician, of this university, to take upon him the principal care of such as fell sick in the hospital, and to lend an helping hand to the physician who was particularly appointed to manage that affair. And this he readily underwent, without the least requital; so that we are not able to make a sufficient return of thanks for so signal an act of charity.

XXXV. In the year 1699, when a malignant fever was raging in these parts, it carried off a great many people; and the hospital lost, on one hand, such men as made it their business to promote its interest;

and on the other, such children as proved the most hopeful of the whole number. It carried off, likewise, several of the schoolmasters that were best qualified for managing the youth; and it grew to that violence, that there was almost a general complain that the usual methods of physic became of no use in this sorrowful juncture of time.

Now these deplorable accidents caused both *sorrow* and *compassion* on our side. *Sorrow*, because frequent changes in such colleges are attended with many unavoidable disorders. *Compassion*, because men were cut off in the very flower of their age, who, by reason of their excellent endowments, seemed very fit to serve the public.

XXXVI. The best remedies being thus baffled by the furious insults of this distemper, there was now no other way left to bear off these sensible trials, but to make an humble application to Him who hitherto had given us so many proofs of the light of his countenance, and of his fatherly care over us. So we united in prayers, and committed to his gracious Providence our sick, who now seemed to be exposed, without any shelter, to the merciless strokes of Death; being mindful, that when the LORD smites a land with a plague, he likewise, out of a tender compassion, commandeth his blessings to go forth, and to support his creatures under their burden. This then made us hope the LORD would make us partakers of his blessing, both that the work once begun, might go on, and not so many youth be swept away in the prime of their blooming years, and before they had employed in this world that talent wherewith he had intrusted them.

XXXVII. Within a month after, GOD was pleased to stir up the heart of an eminent patron, who knew nothing of that distress we here labored under, to communicate to us a specific medicine against the said fever, presenting a receipt of the composition thereof to the hospital; and this he sent very seasonably, just when several persons concerned in the management of the hospital, lay desperately ill, who, within a few days, were happily restored by the use of that medicine.—If a fig be laid on the boil by the command of GOD, it is sufficient.

Since that time, thanks be to GOD, not one soul has been carried off by this violent fever, if the patient was but in a condition to take this medicine. This blessing, which the LORD thus bestowed upon us, has been enjoyed by many others out of the hospital, both in this town, and in other places; and to make this benefit the more general, a paper has been printed on purpose, with an account of the several effects of the said medicine, and directions how to use it.

It was soon observed, that many scrupled to take this kind of physic, moved by a certain maxim of the physicians discouraging the use thereof. Whereupon Providence so ordered it, that Dr. Hoffman, an eminent professor of physic in this university, in a disputation, intitled, *De Diarrhœa in*

Febribus malignis aliisq morbis acutis salutari, has not only made an exact inquiry into the sentiments of physicians in this affair, but also inforced the contrary, by many weighty arguments, drawn both from the writings of the most approved practitioners, and from modern experience; and, § 13, he mentions at large the aforesaid medicine, and the use thereof.

And thus the LORD hath also made good in this point, what the apostle hath left upon record: *He is able to do exceeding abundantly above all we ask or think.* He hath not only put an end to the difficulties which particularly attended the aforesaid disease, but hath furnished us also with several other good medicines in very desperate cases.

XXXVIII. It was, and is like still to prove, a great advantage to us, that the LORD, by a most remarkable Providence, excited certain persons here and there, to such a tender and charitable disposition towards the poor, that they made it as it were their own business to support it, by the most endearing marks of their concurrence. And these I may deservedly call the fathers and mothers of our poor.

I do here not only mean those substantial persons, who generously laid out part of their wealth to relieve the poor, whereof the foregoing account has informed the reader; but also even such as, by reason of the smallness of their estate, were unable to give any thing considerable themselves, yet have left visible tokens of a most tender affection towards the poor, which they did either by the means of good advice, or heart intercession with others; nay, by their own unwearied diligence, and more especially by their fervent prayers to GOD.

I must needs confess, that I have sometimes greatly admired the earnest care, with which the LORD hath inclined some to take a particular survey of the need of the poor, and to support them accordingly. So that I often have remembered St. Paul's saying in such circumstances: *But thanks be to* GOD, *which put the same earnest care into the heart of Titus for you.* 1 Cor. viii. 16. Truly this afforded us no small occasion to praise the Name of GOD.

I know there is no need of making particular mention of such persons as the LORD has been pleased to inspire with so tender a sense towards our poor. True charity keepeth always within the bounds of humility, and doth not in the least affect any applause of men. This then restraineth me from inserting here such instances, especially since I know how apt the world is to pass the worst construction upon such actions. But notwithstanding this, I cannot forbear to take notice in this place, of one particular instance the LORD hath bestowed upon us; and this not out of flattery, or other sinister end, but out of an hearty thankfulness towards a person, who did not receive the least requital, besides our prayers, as long as she lived.

This was the Lady Maria Sophia (Pudewell) Marshall, whom GOD, about the latter end of the past year, and in the fifty-seventh year of her age, hath called to himself. As soon as the first step was made towards the erecting of an hospital, her heart was possessed with such a tender sense of love and kindness, that she looked upon this affair as a business of her own, particularly commited [*sic*] to her trust, and accordingly she took a motherly care for carrying on the same.

To give you a short view of her excellent charity, I must acquaint you, that it was her custom exactly to inform herself what was most wanting in the hospital, and then she considered whether she could procure us any help; which she did by advertising of others, either by letter, or in conference, or by some means or other.

All what she got together, by the blessing of GOD, for the benefit of the hospital, she would set down in writing. If she got any money, she would buy such things which were most wanting, and conveniently to be had in the place where she lived. One time she sent in two hundred shirts for poor children, and part of the linen was woven and whitened at her own charge. And this being down, she would prevail with others to make them up, out of the same principle of charity. The like she did with hats, caps, and other things of that nature; likewise with houshold [*sic*] stuff of pewter, copper, &c.

The pain and trouble she underwent in person is hardly to be paralleled. She was not in the least detered from serving the poor by the uncharitable censures of the world, and she had not the least prospect of getting any outward advantage by it. She was always full of praises and thanksgivings for the blessing the LORD bestowed upon our undertaking, and her letters were indited in the same style.

Her greatest trouble was, that she could do no more for the benefit of the poor; and her greatest joy, when she heard of a new blessing attending us. In the midst of her charitable efforts, she was careful not to send too many poor of her own recommendation, knowing that we already had our complement; and when now and then a poor orphan came in her way, which she took for a proper object of her compassion, before she sent the same to us, she would make a very modest inquiry whether it might be received; as if she had never bestowed the least benefit upon us: neither did she express the least displeasure, nor was her zeal for the hospital at all abated, when she was told, that at present it was impossible for us to accomplish her desire; she being otherwise fully convinced of our readiness to comply with her desire in any thing that lay in our power. And even in the midst of her bodily weaknesses, (which increased the wonder) almost continually oppressing her, and growing more upon her in the latter part of her life, she would not lay aside her usual concern for the hospital. Nay, all her prayers, and very dying speeches, would favor of that tender sense she had for our poor, till she passed out of this into another life.

Now the LORD is not unrighteous, that he should forget the works and labor of her love, which she undertook for his Name's sake; not disdaining to serve CHRIST in his poor members. He had here filled her heart with most ardent flames of love, and now, she having kept her hope to the end, we believe she died in the LORD, and her *works followed her.*

XXXIX. It proved another great furtherance to my design, that the LORD, from the very beginning of the undertaking, had always supported me with the concurrence of such fellow-laborers as sincerely loved GOD and their neighbor. This happily prevented all manner of worldly bye-ends, relating to secular advantage and self-interest, which are more agreeable to the character of an hireling, than of a faithful laborer in CHRIST's vineyard. They have, on the contrary, looked upon this undertaking as a work of GOD, and accordingly have thought their service should be directed to the attainment, not of human applause, but of divine acceptance, in what they underwent for the good of their fellow creatures, even in the midst of many hardships and trials, to which, under a generous self-denial, they themselves have been exposed.

To the same mercy of GOD over us, I intirely ascribe, that all manner of debates, strife, envy, and other sinister practices of that nature, so happily have been prevented amongst them. They have rather borne one another's burden; and not only taken what care they could of the things and persons which have been committed to the particular charge of each of them, but have mutually encouraged one another, when they observed that their fellow-laborer could carry on the affair in which he was engaged to a greater perfection. When I myself have been now and then put upon any thing of hardship, they not only heartily joined with me in prayer, but did whatever they could to ease the burden I was under, one way or other. In this condition of affairs, they had opportunities for the exercise of their faith and charity; and as, on the one hand, they gained much experience, so, on the other, they have been supported by many marks of GOD's loving kindness attending their endeavors. These many spiritual advantages made them not regard the plausible suggestions of certain persons, who under many specious pretences, both by letters and by discourse, endeavored to divert them from the undertaking in which they were engaged.

All the supplies Providence hath so wonderfully bestowed upon us, would have hardly have answered expectation, if, through the gracious Providence of GOD, I had not procured sincere and faithful men for the management thereof. And I must confess, I more admire this branch of GOD's Providence, than the richest mines of silver and gold: and justly enumerate it amongst the means, whereby the whole undertaking has been begun, and thus far carried on. And I do not doubt in the least of GOD's blessing, and good success, so long as he shall vouchsafe us such laborers as impartially consult their consciences, and stand free of that cursed sin of covetousness. While, on the other hand, vain and covetous hirelings would bring nothing but a curse upon the work.

CHAP. III.

Of the many hard trials, under which the Work, through the mighty Protection and Blessing of GOD, hath been carried on.

Footnote from 1787 edition:
The reader will find that the devil is turned commentator. No sooner does GOD display, or make known his promised goodness, but the devil puts his infernal construction upon it, in order to damp the zeal of the instrument that GOD makes use of, and to cut off every supply that should promote and further the cause of GOD.

The malice of the devil, the slander of the world, and the cruel aspersions of secret enemies; that this blessed servant of GOD met with, was [*sic*] enough, one would have thought, to have abated his zeal, and put his faith out of countenance. But he still went on in the LORD's work, relying on the LORD's power, and depending on the LORD's promise, until he compleated it, to the honor of GOD, the comfort of his own soul, and to the confusion of his enemies.

This note is inserted, that the reader may not be discouraged, if he be engaged in the LORD's work; because those who meet with the approbation of the devil, and the applause of the world, have no reward of our FATHER who is in heaven: while, on the other hand, they that expect their reward to be great in heaven, must also expect nothing but reproach from the world, for their labors in the LORD.—Be it so; it only serves to embitter this world the more; and that, in the end, will make heaven the sweeter.

1. BECAUSE many,   for want of sufficient information, have conceived wrong notions of the whole affair, and so missed of the truth; and others, out of what hath been said concerning the manifold admirable proofs of GOD's Providence, might perhaps find themselves prompted to think, that for as much as we have obtained every thing we wanted, after an hearty application to the LORD, the enterprize has been carried on without any trials and difficulties; I think it necessary to set the business in its full light, and to subjoin here a *short account of several hard, and, to flesh and blood, almost insupportable circumstances*, under which the work has lain ever since its first beginning.

Some have been very liberal of their reflections, saying, "That at first this was a work of faith indeed, but now it hath lost that character, there being a sufficient stock provided to carry it on." Others, "That it was no great business for any one to set up an hospital, that had wherewithal to do it." But such men have been absolute strangers both to the frame of my mind, and the circumstances attending the affair, else I am sure they would far otherwise have conceived of this matter.

Though the being furnished with a fund sufficient for the poor, might place a man above the reach of many such trials, yet it would require still a constant care and application to manage it well and faithfully. But what difficulties he is to wade through, that has not the least settled provision, and yet a great many people about him who expect to be fed and cloathed, and furnished with other necessaries, nobody is able to judge, but he that has made the experiment; of which those parents who are obliged to provide but for one poor family, are the most competent judges. He whose cellar and kitchen are stored with all manner of plenty, is quite a stranger to these trials; and human reason doth not see beyond the sphere of things present; whenever these fail, it is ready to give all over for lost.—Faith works best when reason is out of the business.

II. Now such hours of probation, wherein I was reduced to the utmost poverty, have not once, but very often come upon me; in which not only I had nothing, but could not so much as espy any means by which we might be supplied. When I first set myself about this business, I thought that the LORD, in the first onset of poverty, would presently relieve the necessity. But I did not then know the meaning of that expression, *Mine hour is not yet come:* and that Providence now and then traceth such untrodden paths, that human reason is not able to follow. And this proveth a comment upon David's saying; *But thou,* O LORD, *how long?*

95

It has often happened that I had not one farthing left, though the next day the steward was to go to market to buy provision for about three hundred persons.

Now and then I was obliged to pick together such pence and farthings as were laid aside for the benefit of those poor people that beg from door to door.

Such things as were not absolutely necessary, have been turned into money to buy bread.

We happened once to be in the utmost want, when the steward finding me void of all relief, went back with an heavy heart, to see whether he could scrape together two groats, to buy some candles, that the children might not be forced to sit in the dark; and he found nothing till night came on.

And so it has often fallen out, that the steward having given me notice of the present want, has been obliged to go empty away; and I must confess that the frame of my mind was not then perplexed at the want we were in, though by taking share of the burden that the other lay under, I was not a little affected with the crossness of his circumstances. *And such pressing necessities have often afflicted us, till all hope of help and relief was expired, and human reason did not see any manner of probability of being delivered from our straits.*

III. In the extremity of such want and poverty, it has sundry times fallen out, that many of the begging poor, not only in our own neighbourhood, but also from remote places, have very importunately pressed us to make provision for them, as if there had been a great fund of money in my house ready to be distributed. And if I was not able to supply their necessities with a present relief, I needed not think it strange that foul speeches and unkind censures were uttered against me.—This is no wonder, for Israel was ready to stone Moses for bread, when he was in as great want as they.

Nay, in the midst of such trials of want and poverty, there have been persons who attempted at the same time to get from me ten, twenty, an hundred, several hundreds, yea, a thousand, and some thousands of crowns; and when I told them that all this was beyond my ability, I being myself in great straits, they would exclaim against me as void of charity and compassion towards them, and trust in GOD.

Others have forced the poor upon me, without making the least enquiry whether there was any provision in store for their relief. Some of these, whenever it was possible, have been taken in; and some have been sent back, though with great reluctance; unavoidable necessity obliging me to such a procedure.

After we were fully stocked with poor, and utterly unable to receive any more, there were nevertheless some, who by their earnest solicitations to get into the house, wearied me, and put me to a great deal of sorrow and compassion. Nay, I scruple not to say, that the care for those who actually were received into the hospital, was not so heavy upon me, as the pressing importunities of those who were not received, and whose requests I was not able to fulfil.

IV. These difficulties were commonly accompanied with great unthankfulness from many people, which alone had been sufficient to wear out the most resolute patience; especially in one that would make it his business rather to please men, than promote the honor of GOD, and the welfare of mankind. This has been clearly visible in the conduct of some, who not only have been most backward in lending an helping hand towards carrying on so difficult and enterprize, though tending to the common benefit of the town and country; but have also passed the most rash censures upon so useful an undertaking, entertaining many odd suspicions against it, and believing all manner of groundless reports and calumnies thrown upon it; and by such uncharitable proceedings have put me to many difficulties: nay, if I endeavored by lawful ways to procure some help for the hospital, they have bent the whole force of their wit against it.

V. But still greater has been the ingratitude of some, whose children, or those of their relations, have been taken into the hospital out of mere compassion, being reduced to beggarly want and poverty, and maintained at least in schooling, if not also in cloaths, diet, and other necessaries. These now being excited partly by their own malice, partly by the spiteful contrivance and false suggestions of other people, have spread about the country the most abominable reports and imputations, instead of a thankful acknowledgment. One time they would give out, that the children were used more inhumanly in their diet than the very dogs: another time, that they were exposed to the intolerable hardship of incessant labor; whilst such as even pretended to vindicate the management of our affairs, though they would excuse me, did yet lay the blame upon them that were intrusted with the immediate ordering of the children.

By these and the like groundless imputations, the first contrivers whereof have been much countenanced by others of the same disposition, many well-meaning persons have now and then had occasion to enquire into the true state of the affair, and so to put me to the trouble of making many apologies.[21] Not to mention here at large, how often I have been obliged to call to an account those that had any share in the management of the hospital, to know the certainty of the matters called into question; whereby at that time, the business itself they were intrusted with was obstructed, and they themselves sometimes dejected, seeing how little thanks they had for their fidelity.

If at any time a small oversight has happened, or a false step was made, (which now and then will fall out in the management of a family of a far less compass) it was aggravated to the most heinous

---

[21] That is, defenses. (M.S.)

degree, and set forth as most inexcusable and criminal.

VI. But I must not forbear to mention such as having themselves enjoyed the benefit of the hospital, have left the most visible marks of their ingratitude. Children of a profligate life have, by reason of most inveterate ill habits, shaken off all manner of rule and good discipline, and at last run away; and having thus made their escape, have spread abroad a world of lyes, and slanderous reports, to cast the better gloss on their own extravagant and unaccountable proceedings: or if they staid, they have however spun out of their own brains abundance of lyes and calumnies, and communicated them to their mothers, or some other relations; who believing them, without any farther enquiry, have thought it their duty to commiserate their hard usage, and to take them away, and so have spread abroad farther and farther the slanders maliciously contrived by their own children.

From some students also we have received a like treatment. Some being reduced to great want both of maintenance and education, have been taken into the hospital: but irreligion and prophaneness having got so deep footing in some of them, that they baffled all attempts tending to the reformation of their manners, we thought it at last our duty to clear the hospital from the dangerous contagion of so diffusive an evil. As soon as they were removed, they made it their business to cast abundance of aspersions upon it up and down in the country, and so have misled many people into rash and bitter censures, thinking they had reason enough to believe these that had been admitted into the hospital, and were eye-witnesses of many things that had been done there.

VII. But I forbear to set down any more of such uncharitable censures, as have been passed on this charitable undertaking. Those who pretended to be most modest in censuring, and to keep within bounds, would not scruple to accuse us of a *bold presumption* in this affair: and to make good what they alledged, would quote our Saviour's words: *Which of you intending to build a tower, sitteth not down first and counteth the cost, whether he have suffficient to finish it?* Perhaps, because they themselves were never accustomed to extend their trust in GOD beyond their purse, or the ready provision laid up in their vaults or storehouses, they think it strange and unreasonable that others should make greater advances, and arrive at a pitch of confidence in GOD, to which they are altogether strangers. Or because they never were used to commit themselves intirely to GOD's Providence, and to depend upon his assistance, they account it a solecism in conduct to rely rather on the living GOD, than on the uncertain mammon of unrighteousness, whether of themselves or others. As if it was not a much safer way to reckon upon the powerful and infallible assistance of the great Maker of heaven and earth, than to trust to the unstable promises of the wealthy, or have confidence in one's own possessions.

Besides this, they have not well considered what a vast difference there is betwixt a building contrived for the gratifying our own ease and luxury, or expressing our grandeur, as Babylon was by the builders thereof, and one erected merely for the use and service of the poor and distressed people, without any selfish regard to our own ease or satisfaction; the main scope whereof is the glory of GOD. He that engageth in the former, has reason enough to consult his purse; but whoever engages in the latter, may reasonably look for a better and higher Support, even no less than the LORD himself, who must strengthen his faith, and carry him through the powers of darkness, and the oppositions which Satan is apt to raise against it—as well as his children.

VIII. But neither has the building itself escaped the froward censures of ill-meaning people; it being sometimes censured on account of its *bigness*, and sometimes on account of its *magnificence*. Unto such I have answered in short, "I must needs know of what bigness and value the house ought to be, which is necessary to compleat my design.

But in the mean time I assure you, that when the LORD hath finished this house, He will be as able and rich to provide for the poor that are to lodge therein, as he was before." And common reason certainly shews us, that an house which some hundreds of people are to dwell in, must needs be made of a larger compass than a private one.

IX. Others have concerned themselves more than they needed, in expressing their apprehensions, lest my relations, after my death, might attempt to appropriate to themselves such goods as have been brought up for the poor. Whereas they might have more rationally concluded, that I should not fail to preserve these, by the means of a plain testament, from that terrible curse which they would thence draw on themselves by so heinous an act of sacrilege; and thereby to guard them so, as they may not fall under the least censure of unjustly impropriating the goods of others. And though at the present, with approbation of the benefactors, I buy now and then several necessaries under my name, which nevertheless do truly belong to the poor, and which I suppose may have occasioned the aforesaid aspersion; yet there is no want either of public or private records, of such goods as belong to the poor. And now, after all, I take the freedom to observe, that such persons as have themselves bestowed none of their treasure towards the advancement of this hospital, may and ought to leave these concerns to the promoters thereof, who, I suppose, will not be wanting to take care to see their charity employed as it ought to be, and according to their intention.

X. Others again, seeing the undertaking carried on to a pretty good degree, would endeavor to persuade themselves and others, that I was not wearied of it, and wished it had even never been attempted; whereas I do not remember that ever such a thought came into my mind; but on the contrary, meeting therein with so many signal proofs of GOD's Providence, I have found myself, more and more, still encouraged to go on, with my fellow-laborers, in the work so happily begun.

XI. Others have judged, and that perhaps without any ill design, that the management of so many schools and foundations, made for the poor, and the many cares and distractions derived from thence upon me, would hinder my *progress in religion*. But as to this, I can verily assure them, without injuring the truth at all, that as, on the one hand, I never in all my former life obtained such insight into the ways of GOD, as I have done by the help of these manifold trials through which his Providence hath carried me; so, on the other, I never met with better and more frequent opportunities and incitements to the habitual exercise of faith, charity, and patience, wherein, beyond controversy, true and apostolical religion doth consist, than in the circumstances wherein I have been on this occasion.

For my part, I thought it much better to lend an helping hand to my fellow creatures, in imitation of the tender-hearted Samaritan, than to pass by satisfied with an empty speculation, like the priest and the Levite; and I thank GOD that I have learnt how the poor generally stand affected, to which I was a stranger before.

XII. Others have thought the management of so many schools would prove an hinderance to the *pastoral care* I was engaged in; whereas they should rather have concluded, that so vast a number of fellow-laborers, amounting to half an hundred, and more, joining their endeavors in the work of reformation, must needs carry it higher, than if I should preach myself to death, being left alone to manage so important a charge. Besides which I have a curate, who sustains no small part of the pastoral care, and has hitherto answered the character of a faithful, industrious, and watchful minister.

XIII. Besides this, I have observed that many have been influenced to such a degree by the father of lyes, as even to forge many malicious inventions on purpose to hinder our success. Sometimes they would make people believe that whole tuns and waggon loads, or, at least, sacks full of money, were bestowed upon the hospital. At other times, on the contrary, they would say, that *all was spent*, (which often has been true enough:) adding of their own, that now nothing more came in, and our debts were so mightily increased, that we were not able to discharge them, which in a little time must needs prove the final overthrow of the whole affair.

Both these fictions have proved no less injurious than malicious, restraining many well-disposed persons from contributing any farther aid to the hospital, because they either supposed that by reason of so large a provision as was talked of, there was no want of any supply: or else that it would be absolutely in vain to bestow any benefaction upon a work which was ready every hour to come to nothing.

XIV. Nay, the father of lyes has been so impudent in his instruments, as to give out, that many thousand crowns were alienated and perverted to my private interest. That the pope himself, papists, and all manner of sectaries, sent us money. Such and the like stories have now and then been heard to drop even from the mouths of those of whom one would think they should have had more understanding than to believe such ridiculous tales themselves. In fine, I must say, that both *ill* and *well-disposed* persons have been too rash in passing their censures upon the work; the *former* from their own malicious contrivance; the *latter* for want of sufficient circumspection, giving too much credit to groundless reports; by which, though they have not been able to obstruct my proceeding in the work, yet they have indeed created some sorrow in me, and that more upon account of the latter than of the former.

XV. But such and the like contrivances, how spiteful soever, are not to be paralleled with those that assault us nearer home, and which not only have fallen upon me, but likewise (as was hinted before) upon those which joined their hearts and hands with me in this affair. These have been most maliciously charged, that they did feather their own nests with the alms bestowed on the hospital. Whereas I must needs say to the contrary, that they have learned to make shift with a very little; for being all day long employed in the business of the hospital, they have no time left to get their living any other way: and sometimes when in their want they have been relieved by other charitable persons, they have willingly parted with it, to those who were in greater straits than themselves. Nay, some of them have sold their books and cloaths, in case of extreme want, to make provision for the poor.

XVI. How often GOD has supported them in the midst of such trials as generally attend such an undertaking, and raised their sinking spirits above the reach of the outward difficulties they were to pass through, might be made plain by many instances; but, to be short, I shall produce but one.

When the building of the hospital was but just begun, and the workmen employed to carry off the rubbish, the steward, or he who was intrusted with the chief management of the undertaking, met with abundance of difficulties. The laborers one time wanting stones, another time sand or lime, tired him very much with their importunate demands; he not being in a condition then to afford a present supply, because there were neither horses of our own, nor the least appearance of getting any hired for that use, it being just in the height of harvest.

This now very much discouraged him, and cast him into sorrow and perplexity; when finding his thoughts overcast with deep care and concern, he got away into his closet, to be for a while by himself, and in some measure to recollect the scattered powers of his mind. He was but just retired, and venting himself to GOD in sighs and groanings, when the master bricklayer followed him at his heels, and called him back out of his privacy, telling him withal, that stones and other necessaries were immediately to be provided, otherwise the workmen would cease from their work, and yet demand their full pay. This cast him down yet lower; however, away he went with the bricklayer, though he did not know how to break through these difficulties that surrounded him.

When he came to the place where the men were at work, one of the laborers happened to find a piece of coin in the rubbish that was dug up. This he offered to the steward, who took it, and looking upon it, he found the following words impressed thereon:

יהוה׳

Conditor

Condita

Coronide

Coronet

JEHOVAH

the Builder

crown this

MANY HARD TRIALS

Building with a
happy conclusion.

The reading of this inscription raised his sinking
faith to that degree, that with great presence and
readiness of mind he went to work again, hoping
now that he should live to see the building brought
to perfection, though at present, while they were but
breaking up the foundation, we had to encounter
with many difficulties. In the mean time he
contrived a way to get together such necessaries as
the bricklayer had minded him of; and within a few
days it happened that two horses were made over to
us, and some time after, two more, and at last
another, to help forward the building.

The medal was an old piece of coin of the Prince of
Weimar, upon which a friend has made the
following Epigram.

Pauperibus sacras emeret cum Frankius ædes,
Miranda occultis æra reperta locis.
Arcanum cœli prodit res illa favorem,
Et sperare pios optima quæque jubet.
Ipse suis augur spondet bona nummus egenis,
Ut Deus optato sine coronet opus.
Huc affer dum tempus erit, fulvi æris acervos:
Quas dederis, solas semper habebis opes.

When Franck a seat would purchase for the poor,
A wondrous coin was found t' augment his store;

In whose inscription Heav'n's high favors read,
Bid with large hopes the pious rear their head.
GOD's *penny* to his poor is pledge of stores,
And of GOD's hand to crown the work assures.
Then bring your timely offerings in full measure:
Who gives to GOD, can only *keep* his treasure.

XVII. Persons of a worldly mind, being strangers
to such circumstances as these under which the
affair was carried on, both by me and my fellow-
laborers, have now and then sued for some
preferment in the hospital: but when they came to
be informed of the narrowness of our
circumstances, and that our business was managed
without any regard to private interest; nay, that even
those who were engaged in it, must learn to suffer
poverty with the poor; they soon have let fall their
design.

In short, most people have entertained too earthly
thoughts of the business, and have been too apt to
believe it was settled on such a foundation as tended
to the promotion of *secular interest.*

But such and the like things as are managed
under the *Mystery of the Cross*, are better known by
experience than by discourse. If any one endeavors,
in earnest, to support his poor fellow creatures lying
by the way side, in a forlorn condition both of soul
and body, and out of sincere compassion shall help
to bear their burden, how soon will he perceive
himself to lay under a burden heavy enough!

CHAP. IV.

On the Inspection and Direction of the whole Affair.

As for the inspection and direction of the whole undertaking, it is to be observed,

I. That it is grounded upon a *daily conference*, which I hold with those to whom several offices about the hospital are assigned, *viz.* the steward, the inspector of the schools, the physician, the bookseller and apothecary, with the inspector of the students in the hospital. This *conference* is held in the evening, from eight till nine of the clock: though as the business in hand may require, this is occasionally protracted. The reason of pitching on this hour is, that we might not be interrupted in the day time, in discharging our several trusts, and myself in particular, in the pastoral office.

Concerning the conference itself, and the manner of it, it is begun with an hearty prayer; and this being done, each of those who are concerned in carrying on the business, produceth his *memorial*, wherein he has set down in the day such things as he thinks fit to be further considered of; which then are presently brought into debate, and the result thereof, for order's sake, recorded. After we have thus gone through such points as have been proposed

111

to our consideration, and each of us received instructions for the day following, we conclude again the whole conference with a prayer.

II. That care is taken that, if any of our faithful laborers should be absent at any time, all disorders which usually attend such alterations be prevented. To which end we have thought it expedient, that an assistant be allowed to every one that is in any place of trust about the house; who is to lend him an helping hand, and to supply his place, in case of necessary absence.

III. That as for the method of prosecuting the whole undertaking, the following persons are to be considered, *viz.*

1. The director, who upon any emergent occasion is supported by, 2. The curate. 3. The steward. 4. The overseer or inspector of the schools. 5. The physician, who is also intrusted with the inspection over the apothecary's shop. 6. The bookseller, who is fully empowered to order the affairs belonging to that shop. 7. The principal of the students, boarding in the hospital. All these are the usual members of the aforesaid conference.

IV. That the masters of the charity-schools, being thirty in number, hold a weekly conference about the well-ordering and regulating their schools, at the house of the inspector of these schools.

V. That there is, 1. A mistress, or governess, who is intrusted to *govern* the poor girls in the hospital. 2. Another mistress to teach them needle-work, and things of like nature. 3. Another that takes care of washing their linen, and keeping them clean. 4. A nurse to look after the sick. 5. An apothecary. 6. A farmer that manageth the little farm-house at Giebichenstein. 7. The baker, who likewise supplieth the place of a gardener. 8. A taylor: and 9. The rest of the domestics, which are employed in the kitchen, in the wash-house, in cleansing the poor, and in lighting the fires. Likewise the apprentices and hired men in the apothecary and bookseller's shops, and the taylor's shop-board: and, lastly, the people that belong to the aforesaid farmhouse.

Thus much may serve to give a clear apprehension of our affairs, and how they are kept up and carried on in good order, without any distraction of my mind.

CHAP. V.

Of the Advantages which may be expected from such Endeavors.

I. As for the spiritual benefits which may be expected to accrue from such endeavors, and which we are chiefly to regard, they may easily be guessed at, considering the *main scope* of the whole undertaking; which is nothing else but the salvation of souls, and their conversion to life everlasting. Now as the soul is the principal part of a man, and to be managed with much greater care than the body; so the design of the undertaking was never to lay up provision for the body, but this was only used as the means to make a nearer step towards the reformation of the soul.

If any body put another construction on it, and being prejudiced with many groundless suspicions, question the sincerity of our pretensions to that great end, he is desired to have patience till the day comes wherein the LORD will make manifest the counsels of the heart: and so to leave the sentence to GOD, who alone is able to search the most secret recesses of the heart; reserving this as a prerogative most peculiar to himself.

II. In the mean time, I doubt not but persons of candor and unbiassed judgment, may, without much difficulty, penetrate into the bottom of this affair, by taking an impartial survey of the whole method, whereby the work is carried on.

The end we aim at, and the *means* we make use of for obtaining the same, are all of a piece. Whatever is applied to this purpose, tends directly to our great end, without the least digression from it. The means we use are of that nature, that no body can find fault with them under any pretence whatsoever. The *Word of GOD* is instilled into the children from their youth up, and none dare charge us, no not with the least insinuation, that these heavenly oracles are sophisticated either by human traditions, or other erroneous mixtures. Unfeigned *Faith* in our LORD JESUS CHRIST, is laid for a foundation, and a real sense of *Godliness*, attended with a conscientious behaviour, are the most material points; to the obtaining whereof, our earnest endeavors are constantly directed.

As near as is possible, such men are chosen to manage the work of inspection and education, as we can safely rely upon for their candor and integrity, as well as ability, on that behalf; expecting that they will render themselves worthy examples both by their words and their actions. And if it happens that we unexpectedly mistake in our election, the person convicted of any misdemeanor, is obliged to make room for one that is better qualified.

We prevent also, as much as in us lies, the spreading of infectious examples amongst the children, lest they be perverted from the right way. And we take it very kindly, when any body assists us with good advice, how to lay a deeper foundation of the principles of true piety, and of training up children to them. Now such and the like things are known so well, that the most malicious cannot deny it to be so.

III. Two hours are set apart every day, wherein all manner of poor, blind, lame, and impotent persons, both such as live amongst us, and such as come from abroad; as likewise exiles, and such as have lost their goods by fire; and, in a word, all sorts of distressed people, are carefully instructed in the principles of religion, admonished, comforted, and at length supplied with some bodily relief. And this I think every one will allow to be a method useful for the public good.

IV. Many poor orphans, for whose education no body was in the least concerned, and who otherwise of necessity had been drawn away into numberless disorders, and most heinous sins, have been witheld from the dangerous courses which a beggar's life might have exposed them to; and put under good discipline, and instructed in the Word of GOD: whereby in time they may become good Christians, and profitable subjects; which, without question, must turn to the general good of the kingdom.

V. Many boys of good natural parts and endowments, by reason of which they might be made fit for great undertakings, lying hitherto buried under the rubbish ignorance, for want of education, because of their parents poverty, or otherwise, and whose pregnant genius would enable them to become great instruments of mischief to their country, are now found out, and educated for the common benefit, to which they may some time prove useful, by promoting the good and advantage, whether of church or state; which is a thing that deserves the applause of every one.

VI. More free-schools have been set up by occasion of such endeavors, whereby parents reduced to want, and unable to put their children to school, or provide them with necessary books, have an opportunity of sending them where they may be taught gratis; by means whereof many a youth, who would otherwise abandon himself to the government of sensual and brutish lusts, is, as it were, plucked out of the jaws of Satan, and instructed in the principles of religion, and other useful learning; so that he himself reapeth the benefit of the school where he is bred, and the commonwealth, a well qualified member.

VII. And what else may such foundations be more properly accounted, than *seminaries* set up for the general good of the country? Here a foundation is laid for training up good workmen in all trades; good school-masters; nay, good preachers, and counsellors; who of course hereafter will think themselves the more obliged to serve every one, because they have both an experimental knowledge of GOD's Providence from their youth up, and the benefit of a sound and solid education. And this may put sovereign magistrates in good hopes, that from such and the like endeavors, may proceed the best and most faithful subjects, fitted for their service, who also may prove instrumental, in due time, to retrieve others from their vicious course of life.

VIII. By such undertakings therefore the country will be cleared by degrees of stubborn beggars, thieves, murderers, highwaymen, footpads, and the whole pack of loose and debauched people, who, as we may find, if we search into the true reasons of such overflowing wickedness, commonly let loose the reins to disorder and impiety, because they never imbibed so much as the least tincture of a good education. Now an undertaking of this kind, may prove a real foundation of putting some stop to the fierce torrent of such headstrong vices, and so conduce both to the spiritual and temporal good of the whole country.

IX. Farther; whereas by such charitable endeavors for the solid education of youth, not only a world of such and the like mischiefs are prevented, and a foundation laid, whereon a new structure of a reformed life may be raised up; but also by such visible instances of alms well bestowed, many may be encouraged the more willingly to contribute their charitable assistance towards the support of so necessary a work, who perhaps could not be otherwise induced thereto by the most persuasive rhetoric, without such real demonstrations of the benefit proposed: it is manifest that the management of such an affair as this may prove no small help to magistrates, for the better regulation of such attempts, whenever they may think fit to engage themselves therein. As for the people, they will, by such charitable foundations, come to be melted down more and more into a gentle and charitable temper of mind; and have the untractableness and stubbornness of their natural disposition mollified by mutual acts of charity; which will take off much trouble from the magistrate, by preventing those disorders, which sometimes cannot be suppressed without great care and application.

X. It is moreover a means to wear off, at least in some measure, that *stain* which the Christian religion hath contracted in these our unhappy days, *viz.* that there is such a crowd of poor helpless people in the midst of those who stile themselves *Christians*; whereas the LORD requires of his people, that there should be no poor amongst them. Hence it is no small honor to a city or country, if the poor be regularly ordered and maintained.

ADVANTAGES OF SUCH ENDEAVORS

XI. The prayers of poor fatherless children, and of all such as enjoy the benefit of hospitals, are the strongest wall and fortress to defend a city and land from the invasions of any adversary; as, one the contrary, the tears or sighs of poor distressed people, who commonly express their grievances in that manner, when they lay neglected under extreme necessity, draw down the dreadful displeasure of Almighty GOD against that unhappy nation wherein such cruelty is practiced.

XII. A great many students, partly by being kept under a strict discipline themselves, partly by being every day employed in teaching the children, are prepared for a skilful management of schools up and down in the country. And having been used to a good and exact method, they may prove instrumental to effect, in some measure, the reformation of schools, which is so necessary at this time; especially if they should happen to get into parsonages, or parochial cures, and so come to be intrusted with the particular inspection of schools.

XIII. As the whole university here has been set up for the real good of our church and state, so this general good is so far advanced by means of the undertaking, as the number of students in the university has been not a little augmented thereby. Now the number of students freely maintained in the hospital, amounts to fifty, sixty, seventy, nay, sometimes eighty, all together at one time; not to mention those who, in expectation of such a benefit, come hither; which must needs make a considerable addition to the number of students in divinity.

XIV. What spiritual benefits the city of Hall in particular, and Glaucha in the suburbs, have reapt from this foundation, is sufficiently known, and no body can deny, unless those whose judgments are darkened and corrupted by bitter envy, or rank atheism, so as to render them stupidly insensible of a work, whereby not only many fatherless children are brought up to the glory of GOD, but also a way found out whereby poor people, both old and young, in the city and suburbs, may arrive to a competent knowledge of Christian principles, not only by public, but private instructions; there being several schools erected for this purpose.

In such parts of the parish as are farthest off from the common schools, because it would be difficult for children to go every day so far, particular schools have been set up nearer their respective habitations, and all pretences cut off, which parents might alledge to excuse their backwardness in sending their children to school. If they are unable to pay for schooling, they may send them to a free-school, where any child is provided with books, paper, and other necessaries. Which is another benefit redounding to the city and country by these endeavors.

XV. No body has reason to think that these advantages, which have been hinted at, are only the evaporations of an idle brain, without any real ground of hope to enjoy them in time to come. For according to the common sense of mankind, one may easily judge, that as a tree but newly planted, cannot bring forth a full crop of fruit in its first years, so these endeavors, which were begun but about six years ago, cannot arrive to any considerable degree of perfection, nor produce those happy effects in so small a space of time, which may hereafter be expected. Yet in the mean while, I assure the reader, that the LORD hath given us already so many proofs of his blessing, that we have no reason, when we cast an eye upon the first fruits, to hope less hence than the afore-mentioned advantages and benefits. Not to mention now, that one may confidently foretel the event of such things, if the *means* designed for obtaining the *end* be rightly applied. What else could inspire us with courage to attempt any good thing? But while I thus speak, I do not deny that human infirmities, and even scandalous abuses, may too frequently insinuate themselves into the best-contrived projects. Many a plant perhaps may be nipped in the bud.

XVI. Besides these spiritual advantages redounding to the public, and which we have reason to hope for, we may also easily discover several outward or accidental benefits, likely to be the result of such an undertaking. Thus many a poor workman has got his living whilst the house was building. Many a poor student has been supplied with some relief: and who can deny, that it must needs tend to the good of a place, where all the domestics, servants, and apprentices, are used to a godly and orderly way of living, as they are in the hospital; there being every where so great a want of pious and faithful servants. Many a beggarly child is now educated in such a way, that he hereafter may get his own livelihood, and so prove serviceable to others, to whom he would have been a burden, if he had without restraint pursued the course he was engaged in. Many a poor widow, being reduced to the utmost straits, and not knowing where to get any relief for her children, is readily supplied, and the children brought up with greater care, than perhaps their own fathers would ever have done.

XVII. And in fine, every one, I think, will confess, that a town or country is so much the more abundantly blessed with temporal advantages, by how much the more effectual care is taken for the maintenance of the poor; experience itself bearing witness, that those governments are the most flourishing, which concern themselves most to provide well for the poor.

CONCLUSION.

THIS, beloved reader, is the account of the hospital and other charity-schools, which I would at present sincerely offer to your consideration, in order to promote the honor, praise, and glory of GOD, the Giver of all good, and to encourage my fellow creatures in faith and charity. I have studied brevity as much as I could, and only set down such things, as I thought might prove the most serviceable for the edification of the reader. I mean, that he may magnify the LORD, and that every lover of truth may be rightly informed of what has been hitherto done in this affair.

In the account itself, to the best of my knowledge, I have neither wronged nor flattered any person whatsoever, though I had a fair opportunity to have done both. Hence I may with good reason require every reader to give an unreserved credit to what has been delivered here. I am in good hopes that many a person, who thinks it worth while to peruse these sheets, will, for the future at least, restrain himself from all rash censures, and repent, if he has in any respect judged before the time. Likewise, that many, by reading these endearing proofs of the infinite love and goodness of our great GOD, will find no small ease and comfort in the midst of their dismal circumstances, exciting them to run with greater courage the race that is set before them. If that be in any degree the result of this account, I shall be very well satisfied with such a blessing.

But if it should happen that some, in reading over these papers, find themselves prompted cheerfully to second our endeavors with some actual contribution, and lay out some of the generous efforts of their charitable inclinations, towards the education of poor children; I here assure the reader, that it is rather an effect *accidentally* resulting from hence, than a thing directly proposed to myself in the publication of this narrative.

I would have no person upon the face of the earth, let him be ever so great, eminent, wealthy, pious, or well-inclined, think that I put my trust in him. The LORD, by numberless proofs of his veracity, hath most clearly demonstrated, that this honor is due to Him alone; and that I am in gratitude bound to depend on Him with intire confidence, (and O that He, by His SPIRIT, would more and more enable me to do this!) and keep from idols. In the midst of the greatest trials, he hath impressed a lively sense of that word upon my mind: *Rectius ad Patrem quam ad fratres.* "It is better having recourse, in the time of tribulation, to the FATHER, than to the brethren." For all they that *look unto Him, and their faces are not ashamed.* Psalm xxxiv. 5. And the LORD hath taught me also, by happy experience, the truth of what follows in the next verse: *This poor man cried, and the* LORD *heard him, and saved him out of all his troubles.*

I hope that such as fear GOD, will not brand me with ingratitude for the plainness of my speech, nor be offended with me that I do not rely upon them, but upon GOD. The acts of charity performed by any one in the LORD's work, are far more noble and endearing, if they be done in singleness of mind, and offered up with a sincere regard to the honor of GOD, and the benefit of our fellow creatures. It is the character of true love, not in the least to be puffed up in regard to its charitable deeds, but to let them sink into oblivion, like a sacrifice wholly consumed by the fire of the altar; confiding intirely in CHRIST JESUS, and seeking after nothing but to increase, from the fulness of CHRIST, the inward power and vigor of the spiritual life; laying under a deep sense of its own unworthiness, that so it may unite itself nearer and nearer to Him, who is the Giver of all good gifts.

In short, if I should go about to enumerate all the happy effects which, both at home and abroad, have resulted from the example of our endeavors in this affair, they would require a particular treatise by themselves. But at present, I think I have sufficient reason to forbear to insist any farther upon that subject. In the mean time, the LORD hath fully assured me, that the world will never be able to suppress them. The LORD, I am sure, will water this his lily, that it may still more and more diffuse the fragrancy of its smell. For the LORD liveth, and praised by GOD, who is my Hiding-place: and let the GOD of my Salvation be exalted. *Hallelujah!*

A
CONTINUATION

OF THE ACCOUNT OF THE
FOOTSTEPS
OF
Divine Providence,
IN THE
ERECTING and MANAGING the HOSPITAL
at GLAUCHA without HALL.

In a LETTER to a FRIEND.

DEAR FRIEND IN CHRIST,

BECAUSE you are desirous to know how our undertaking concerning the *Charity-schools*, and especially the *Hospital* lately erected, hath been carried on, since the narrative thereof was communicated to the public, *viz.* from the beginning of the year 1701, to the end thereof; I have here, for your satisfaction, sent you a farther account of these transactions; considering, that as such a discovery of GOD's mercy may redound to the glory of our great Creator and Preserver, so the unfathomable goodness of GOD, laying such a strong obligation upon me, hath been no small incitement to me to run over such wonderful *Footsteps* thereof, as have been hitherto traced out in our view; and at the end of the year, to make within myself an exact survey of the manifold and illustrious proofs of his Providence; that so all the mercies of GOD may first in myself produce the effects for which they have been conferred on me. And since you write, that by such a narrative as I might give you of these matters, not only yourself may, in probability, reap some spiritual benefit, but it may also redound to the good of others; I heartily approve of your desire; not regarding the uncharitable censures of some, who are apt to reject the most evident demonstrations, whereby their prejudices against the affair might be removed, and so are ready to charge that with selfishness, which hath been delivered here for the glory of GOD.

Now, though there is no occasion for any such precautions in regard of you, to whom I direct this letter, (your integrity being fully known unto me) yet I have thought them necessary in respect of others, into whose hands this letter may possibly fall; since I not only give you the liberty to communicate it to any that shall desire it of you, but am also resolved to get it here printed, as a *Continuation* of that Narrative which heretofore hath been published upon the same subject.

I testify then, on my conscience, before that GOD who searches the heart and the reins, that I have not knowingly delivered any thing, even of the smallest moment, that may be charged with untruth, either in the substance of the business, or in the circumstantials thereof: which I am ready to make out by most evident, and (in such things as fall under the apprehension of human sense) even by *ocular demonstrations*, if that should ever appear necessary. These things are not carried on in secret, but are exposed to every one's view; and no body can question the truth of what is here said, unless he be altogether a stranger in these parts; for those that are upon the place, must wilfully shut their eyes, if they would impeach me of falshood in a thing daily obvious to their sight: and as for such circumstances as are not apparent to their sight, they may easily be made otherwise sufficiently sensible of the reality of them.

The foregoing *Narrative* was occasioned, as has been mentioned, by a commission, given out by his Prussian Majesty, to take an exact view of the whole state of this present business concerning the care of the poor. And this was done by four of his pivy [*sic*: privy] council. Those that were prejudiced against the undertaking itself, began to rejoice at this commission, in hopes that it would prove an overthrow of the whole affair, or at least, after some while, bring it to a stand, especially because the commission was not ordered at my request, and so would, in probability, be the less favorable to me. This spiteful expectation was seconded with abundance of lyes, which were spread about even before the coming out of the commission.

When I was under these circumstances, I drew up an account of the rise, progress, and wonderful preservation of the undertaking, and not only laid it before his Majesty's commissioners, but answered also what they asked me by word of mouth, with presence of mind, and a sincere dependence upon GOD. These delegates are still alive, and were much pleased with the account they received at that time; not only testifying their satisfaction to me, but offering also a most favorable relation of it to his Majesty. And now the opposers were silenced, and a sudden damp cast on their joy; and I wish they had been affected also with a due remorse for their former guilt.

As soon as this business was over, I digested the most material points, of what was delivered to the said delegates, into an *historical account*, and presented it to the public.

Wherefore I believe I may with confidence conclude, that no reasonable person can, with any plausible pretence, question my candor in this affair: which whoever shall continue to do, he gives plain demonstrations of his being biassed by partiality, in attempting still to pass an arbitrary and censorious judgment on a thing, which not only has been justified by sovereign authority, but also cleared by such manifest proofs, as are sufficient to bear down all contradictions of the gainsayer.

It is true, I am surrounded with many, who, to my knowledge, do not in the least favor my design; but examining into the true reasons, I find these is none, but an overfondness of their own dull *lifeless* religion, valuing themselves upon a fair shew of *dead* formality, willing to pass for good Christians, though never found at the bottom; and this makes them reject such principles and proceedings as, they apprehend, would bring religion too near home.

Would it not be an audacious attempt for me, (which it is almost incredible that any one should ever charge me with) to go about the contrivance of so many forged reports, for the space of seven years, to persuade others, both by word of mouth and in writing, of the truth of them, to abuse the authority of a royal commission for colouring the design, nay, even to put such things in print, if truth itself was not on my side? And if it were possible for any of these biassed persons any way to convict me of so much as one falshood, how readily would he lay hold on every opportunity to sift out the least untruth, imposed upon the magistrates, or others of my fellow Christians. But now I can challenge all the world, and confute the impudence of those that rail against me with scurrilous pamphlets, by laying down some plain and ocular demonstrations of the present state of our whole affair.

The hospital is actually set up, and the number of children, students, and necessary officers, constantly maintained therein, amounts to more than two hundred. As for the building itself, hitherto it has required a vast deal of charge, to bring the inside thereof to its full perfection. Besides which, there are also erected several schools for the benefit both of poor boys and girls, who are maintained apart. Not now to mention several other things, and the sick and indigent of the hospital, upon whose account daily expences are required.

My neighbours very well know that I have no abundance of this world's goods, (though a Christian may enjoy all in GOD and CHRIST) call them moveables, or immoveables, or what you will, no, not so much as would maintain a small family; much less have I such an estate as might suffice both to maintain so many poor, and to erect an house for their reception. This consideration, I think, might prove a powerful inducement to all, to give the honor to GOD, and to acknowledge that it is *His Work*, and not to be attributed either to me, being but a miserable worm, or any other creature in the world whatever; but only to Him *who alone is the Most High, the Creator of all, the omnipotent and terrible King, who sitteth upon his throne judging right.* He alone has done all this, and promoted it from the first rise till now, by his fatherly blessing; and indeed not out of a great stock laid up before hand, as some have given out, but out of nothing he hath made something, according to his infinite mercy, supporting the faith and resolution of so poor a creature as I am; insomuch that I did not rely on any worldly wealth, but only on the arm of the LORD, *who is able to do exceeding abundantly above all that we can either ask or think*; and this made me not to scruple the truth and certainty of *things not seen*.

I have run the hazard of depending upon this gracious GOD, and by obtaining good success, have learnt the value of that expression, *None that wait on Him are ashamed:* and I hope I shall further succeed in Him, to confound the unbelief of those that think themselves safer in a large provision of mammon, than in the living GOD, who yet is able to deliver from death. Thus the spirit of incredulity being discomfited, and put to shame by the work of the LORD, has not in store any manner of weapon to lift up against it, but slanders and calumnies; a vein of malice and envy running through all its actions, so as to brand with the imputation of untruth, things as clear as the sun at noon day, or to cry down the praises and acknowledgments flowing from a sense of GOD's goodness, as the mere result of pride and ostentation. I hope, in the mean time, our great and good Creator, owning these small beginnings, however contemptible they may appear to the world, will not fail powerfully to carry them on: and that He will confound more and more the restless spirit of infidelity, with its whole retinue of lyes and slanders. Wherefore, whoever will obstinately persist in his unbelief, he may run this hazard at his own expence, till he find by experience that the LORD will, in spite of all opposition, do what pleaseth him: and by the loud fame of his wonderful work, awaken many thousand souls out of their lethargic sleep of unbelief, strengthen them in faith, support them under trials and probations, excite them to praise his Name, and transform them into his likeness, by infusing into them the Spirit of love, of power, and of a sound mind, through such tender and endearing marks of his goodness as we have enjoyed.

Of this he hath given us many signal proofs, since the first Narrative of the Undertaking, reaching to Easter 1701, has been published. This proved a means, whereby the LORD was pleased to confer many a blessing on many souls; for which I offer up a joyful Hallelujah to his Name. And this encourages me to hope, that this present letter to you, will be attended with the same benediction. *My soul shall make her boast in the* LORD: *the humble shall hear thereof and be glad.*

But now for your farther information, you must know, that the whole undertaking hath been hitherto carried on as it was first begun. Less than twenty shillings (as hath been said in the foregoing account) was the first fund of erecting a *charity-school*; by the help whereof, a parcel of poor vagrants was taken in, and only furnished with books and schooling at free cost.

This was the meal in the barrel which hath not been wasted, and the oil in the cruse that hath not failed to this day. This was the fund that produced *four* charity-schools, which constantly have been supported. These charity-schools occasioned a farther project to set up an *Hospital*; I being fully convinced of its necessity, though I had nothing to do with it withal. Another good effect it had was, the maintenance of *poor scholars*; as it was desired by a person who gave five hundred crowns towards defraying the charges thereof.

The well-spring of the Divine bounty hath ever since been flowing: and may it still pour forth its most plentiful emanations, that many more young students, of mean condition, may draw comfort and support from thence; which I believe, in great assurance, the LORD will fulfil.

When at first we wanted but a little house, by reason of the small number of our children, then I resolved, in the Name of GOD, to buy one, and the LORD readily supplied me with so much money as I wanted for that purpose. This house served our turn till necessity required a bigger; and when this was thought necessary, there was one purchased, and the LORD furnished us with a suitable sum of money. But when this likewise was found insufficient, and the hiring of houses scattered up and down through the town, was apt to create not small disorder, we resolved, in the *Name of GOD*, to lay the foundation for a competent building. The LORD knoweth we had not so much as would answer the cost of a small cottage, much less such a building as might hold two hundred people. Neither were there wanting such as discovered the rough and difficult ways we were like to pass through, if I would pursue the design. Others advised to set up an house of wood, to save the expensive cost of a stone building. So again some would say, *What is this waste for?* And by such, and the like arguments, I was almost prevailed on to comply. But the LORD strengthened my faith with so powerful a conviction, as if he had said expressly unto me, *"Build thou it of stones, and I will pay the charge."* Indeed He hath been as good as his word: and from week to week, from month to month, the crumbs, as it were, of his comfort, have dropped down, and fed our poor, as one feedeth a brood of tender *chickens.* So that neither have the orphans suffered want, nor the workmen been exposed to any hardship, through the defect of their wages.

Nothing of what the LORD hath bestowed upon us is turned into a *fund*, but laid out according to the present necessity. What trials we have gone through, under the several emergencies of these affairs, hath been explained by many instances; and they are still carried on under the like circumstances, there being no settled provision which we could reasonably depend upon.

The public collection, which, by authority of his Prussian Majesty, was to be made throughout his dominions, was never set on foot but in a few provinces; and in this juncture of time, I have given it quite over, that so I might cut off all manner of slanders, which some would raise against the design, from the execution of that grant. But notwithstanding all this, not one of the orphans, nor any such as are employed about them, have had any reason to complain of want; so that if ever they should be asked, *Did ye lack any thing?* they must needs say, *Nothing.* Luke xxii. 35.

It is true, that I have been very often reduced to the last extremity, both in this and the foregoing years, so that I had not one crown, nay, not one groat left. But as the LORD hath at all times relieved us with seasonable supplies, so He hath now carried us through the trials of this year with his usual Providence, and my soul hath found rest in Him, the great Creator of heaven and earth.

Just when the foregoing narrative was prepared for the press, twenty crowns were sent, by one that lived at a great distance, which proved a seasonable support. The next week, when all was spent, an unexpected help of fifty crowns was sent in, by a person from whom I little expected any such thing. But this not serving our turn, fifty more fell in from the kindness of a patron; wherein this was remarkable, that whereas this gentleman was wont to allow this sum at the beginning of the year, by a journey he undertook, having been hindered this year from performing his promise at that particular time, he sent it now in a more seasonable hour, when we were reduced to greater want.

Soon after this, a certain lady offered to bestow every year as much salt as the hospital wanted. No sooner had she resolved on this, but another was moved hereby to send some corn for the benefit of the hospital.

Besides this, their fell in now and then some small sums; but these proving insufficient for carrying on the work, by the Providence of GOD we received a thousand crowns, which were left to the hospital in the foregoing year by the will of a deceased benefactor; but the payment thereof was put off till now, and we were glad to have it at so seasonable a juncture.

A gentleman about the same time offered twelve crowns; and a widow sent a ducat out of her small stock. Others were still contributing something or other to our support, being such as were for the most part *unknown* to me, or at least would have their names *concealed*.

About June our stock beginning again to decay, a person, who would not be known, presented us with twenty-five crowns. And another, who was a favorer of the hospital, bestowed forty crowns upon it: as also a gentleman sent twenty more, which some time before he had offered to pay yearly: moreover, a certain general paid down the sum of an hundred crowns; which was also followed with a gift of six, sent by a professor of divinity, bearing this inscription written upon a paper:

> "These little mites bestowed are,
> Upon the objects of GOD's care."

A CONTINUATION OF THE ACCOUNT

But (O how faithful is GOD!) when all this was not sufficient to defray the necessary charges, I just then received two letters of advice by the post: in one whereof I was told, that two hundred and fifty crowns should be paid down for the relief of the hospital. This sum came from a certain doctor of physic beyond sea, who ordered the payment thereof here. *The* LORD *be his physician!* It seems that he understood something of the High-Dutch[22] language, and he wrote to the merchant, whom he appointed to pay the money, that if he could not send it immediately, he should give me notice; "For," saith he in his letters, "he is in daily want, and I am sure he will quickly send for it."

This indeed gave me no small encouragement: for I thought, The LORD will rather excite some good souls beyond sea to assist us, than to let us suffer any want.

The other letter of advice promised seventy crowns, which were collected, far from the place, in a *charity box*, by some friends, for the relief of the hospital. The same box has farther supplied us with money twice this year; at one time with the sum of fifty crowns, and at another with sixty.

Before this was spent, a patron sent ten ducats in gold, and ten crowns more in smaller money; and the person by whose hand it was brought, made an addition of thirty crowns more.

---

22 That is, German. (M.S.)

THE FOOTSTEPS OF DIVINE PROVIDENCE

At the end of June, a benefactor, who had engaged himself to pay twelve crowns yearly, sent in six at the half year's end, and this came at a very seasonable hour. Soon after, six ducats, and six crowns were sent; the latter whereof a maiden gentlewoman had ordered, in her last will, to be paid to the hospital; who also, besides this, bequeathed the sum of an hundred crowns to the hospital; fifty whereof were delivered to me at a time when the *last farthing* was spent; which gave me a fresh instance of the wise Providence of GOD, whereby every thing is disposed in its proper time.

I cannot but take notice here, that the LORD hath been often pleased, even from the first beginning of the work, to make two benefits out of one. First, he hath stirred up a benefactor to confer something on the poor, which at that time hath been intimated to us, either by letter, or by word of mouth; but the money itself hath not been paid till some time after. And Providence hath so ordered it, that the promised money came at a juncture, wherein our extreme want rendered us the more sensible and grateful for the benefit received. This has taught me not to repine, though the actual payment of the money promised has a while been delayed: for experience hath convinced me, that it is safely kept in the hands of the LORD, who bestoweth it when *his hour is come*; not regarding always the time which we proposed to ourselves, because the weakness of our faith often makes us long for it before the time we want it. GOD hereby justly claims to himself our whole dependence, and disengages us from idolizing the promises of men: for though they are both able and willing to give something for the support of the poor, yet the actual performance of it dependeth upon the will of GOD. *He spake, and it was done, He commanded, and it stood fast.* Psalm xxxiii. 9.

I cannot forbear mentioning here, to the praise of GOD, and humble acknowledgment towards our Sovereign, that when the two thousand crowns, which his Prussian Majesty was graciously pleased to bestow upon the hospital, were delivered to me, (one thousand whereof was a free gift of his Prussian Majesty, and the other was discounted out of the excise, to the undertaker of the building, who was otherwise to have paid so much) it happened to be just in a time wherein we labored under many vast expences, which were required both for paying the workmen, and defraying other necessary charges, which at one time ran up higher than at another.

Blessed be the wonderful dispensation of GOD in these wise dispositions of things! May it be his good pleasure to bless his Majesty's government, and to inspire him with an hearty zeal, always to promote all manner of praise-worthy undertakings; that from thence he may reap joy and satisfaction, whenever, under the happy influence of Heaven, GOD's work is carried on with success.

In July, a traveller happened to come hither, and by the sight of the hospital, found his charity so far excited, that he readily offered five ducats in gold.

A friend of ours having purchased two silver mines, in the mine-works near Freiburgh, called the New Blessing, and having improved them for the benefit of the hospital, sent now two crowns as the result thereof.

Last summer the LORD inclined also the heart of his Royal Highness Prince George of Denmark, residing in England, bountifully to disburse the sum of three hundred crowns for the hospital, which, by a bill of exchange, was sent hither. The LORD remember this benefit! I must say, that this support, coming from abroad, proved a fresh instance, both of the admirable Providence of GOD, and of his perpetual care for our relief. How easily are the rash censures of *unbelieving* men confounded, by such unexpected proofs of the gracious dealings of GOD! Nothing dropped from their lips but such and the like expressions, "The work cannot hold out, because there is no settled fund for it." But is not GOD the most stable and the *most certain fund?* Or will they set up a competition betwixt GOD and mammon, to discover whether is the most *constant?* Is not heaven better *fixed* than any terrestrial bottom wherein they would found themselves? And is not our GOD the great Creator of heaven and earth, and an universal Monarch indeed, having full power to dispose of all the treasures of the whole world, in what manner he pleaseth? But for my part, I must confess, I reap a particular comfort out of such rash expressions as these, which are the spawn of unbelieving hearts. For upon occasion thereof I am the more inclined to believe, that the LORD will *vindicate* his honor against such presumptuous persons.

I add only this, that I never as yet have missed my aim, when I have undertaken any thing in dependence upon the LORD; but relying upon men, and their assurances, I have met with abundance of disappointments, and that sometimes without any fault of theirs. If one spring happened to be stopped up, another was opened instead thereof. From whence we may justly infer, that GOD *alone is the most powerful, and the most certain Support.*

But to return. After this we were again reduced to some necessity, and then a countess sent in about twenty-five crowns, with this direction upon a paper: "According to the order of the KING of Kings, these five-and-twenty crowns are sent to the poor in sincerity of heart." In another place a lady had vowed, that if she should be happily delivered, she would then bestow fifty crowns upon the hospital, which was done accordingly; and these fifty crowns were attended with about twelve more, sent by another hand.

Another time, when our stock was very low, there was sent into the house, by one who would not make himself known, a blue cloak, a furred cap, and one crown in money; the latter being put up in a bit of paper, with these words, "The LORD JESUS increase it to thousands of thousands, even like the stars of heaven in number, and as the sand of the sea in multitude, and make the fruit of Righteousness grow up from generation to generation."

Almost about the same time, a widow sent ten crowns, with this direction, "Out of a sincere heart this small portion is sent. There will be a blessing upon the widow's mite."

At this time also a certain person was, upon some occasion, fined in the sum of one hundred crowns, by his Prussian Majesty, and ordered to pay in the same to the hospital; upon whose intercession, one half thereof being remitted, the other was readily paid down.

Another time, all our money being spent, I met a young lawyer in the street, who told me that he himself was a poor orphan, but that the LORD had wonderfully provided for him, which induced him to remember our poor, and so he presented me with a rose-noble.[23]

A certain countess, when our treasury was very low, sent in about twenty-four crowns; and about twelve crowns more came from an unknown hand.

---

[23] An old English coin of sixteen shillings and eight pence.

A CONTINUATION OF THE ACCOUNT

About Michaelmas our want was exceeding great, as it usually falleth out in that season; this juncture of time requiring vast expences, both for cloathing the children, and providing wood against winter; as also for discharging such debts as are contracted before Michaelmas fair, that being the usual time of payment with us. But the LORD, according to his wonted goodness, carried us through all these difficulties. For a certain minister, out of one of the chiefest Hanse Towns, sent fifty crowns. As also a certain count, having taken a view of the hospital, presented it with an hundred crowns: and another person, whose name I know not, and who had engaged to pay down, every Michaelmas, thirty crowns, sent in the same at this time very seasonably: not now to mention other small sums of four, ten, twenty, twenty-four crowns, &c. then bestowed on us.

It was remarkable farther, that the steward being much concerned for getting some new linen for the hospital, about Michaelmas, was happily supplied by the liberality of a nobleman, who sent in eighteen pieces of linen cloth for the benefit of the poor. But the boys being still in want of neckcloths, and the steward much concerned how to procure them, as knowing the little money we had by us, was to be laid out for other necessaries of greater importance, it so happened, that a well-disposed person came hither, and readily supplied both the boys with neckcloths, and the girls with caps; which made our steward once more deeply sensible of the goodness of GOD, this being a farther proof that he had unnecessarily disquieted himself with anxious thoughts.

For several weeks in the harvest, and about the beginning of winter, we met with a wonderful train both of sorrowful trials, and joyful deliverances, ordered for us by Divine Providence. For though a certain minister of *W.* sent in twelve crowns, acquainting us withal that an unknown person had designed them for the hospital, who desired in the mean time the prayers of our poor, in a certain concern they were then engaged in, (wherein also I hear the LORD hath graciously granted our request;) and though the rector of a school offered us six crowns in ready money, and six more by a bill of exchange; besides some other small sums falling in; yet all this seemed too little to carry us through the present want.

About the same time I wrote to you, my dear friend, as you may remember, that the undertaking still went on in the same manner, without the least settled provision (as they call it, who generally labor under abundance of cares, in the midst of their plentiful revenues) for the maintenance of the hospital, it being supported only by such gifts as the LORD was pleased to bestow upon us day after day; and that I then had but a few crowns left. Likewise, probably, you may remember that you wrote me word, "It is strange to see that the affair is still carried on in the same way; and I take this for a good omen, thinking that you are more happy under these, than any other circumstances." When I received this letter, I had then but fifteen pence in store: but soon after I had read your letter, a student came, and told me of some body, whose name he would not tell, who sent for the support of the hospital, forty crowns in silver, and five ducats in gold. He desired only a receipt, which while I was writing, a godly minister from *M.* came to see me, and praised the LORD, when he heard after what manner our want was just then supplied; offering me at the same time a parcel of silver lace, which a gentlewoman at *B.* now growing sensible of her vanities, had given him for the relief of our hospital, she having ript them off from her fine cloaths, wherewith she heretofore usually endeavored to set herself out in the eye of the world, with positive order that we should not sell it till we had burnt it, for fear that some body else would apply it to the same ill use of gratifying their pride.

But all this was soon spent, in that extremity to which we were reduced. And just when the last penny of our stock was laid out, a packet came to my hands by the post, containing about sixty crowns, which was delivered in so seasonable an hour, that I sent the packet itself to the steward, as soon as it was handed to me, he being then in great want of money.

But now I was again as poor as before, and so little help was brought in this week, that one Friday, when the steward, according to custom, came to me for money, I had but a crown to give him. The very same evening I happened to tell the overseer of the building, "You must bring me money to-morrow, for my stock is quite exhausted." In the mean time, the steward again importuned me for money. I told him he had received the last crown yesterday, and I had not a farthing left. He asked, what he should do with the man that used to cleave the wood, and the women that cleaned the children; for being poor people, they would sadly want their money: adding, "If there is but one crown to be had, I will make shift." I replied, "There is not so much now in store; but the LORD knows it is an hospital for the poor, and that we have nothing for its maintenance."—"It is true," says he; and so away he went pretty comfortable. Coming within sight of the hospital, he saw a waggon before it, laden with corn, which one of our benefactors had caused to be conveyed thither, (knowing nothing of the want we then were reduced to;) at which sight the steward was surprized with joy, exceedingly admiring the wonderful Providence of GOD. Yet he had still the forementioned concern upon him, *viz.* how to get a little ready money for the aforesaid poor people, who had been employed in the hospital. In the mean time it sell out, that besides some remnants of cloth, and some children's stockings, five crowns were sent by a merchant, and delivered to *him*, whom I bade the night before to bring me some money; who then readily supplied the want of the steward, with as much as would suffice to pay the cleaver of the wood, and the women that cleaned the children. The rest he brought unto me, rejoicing like a child that he now was able to bring me some money, as I bade him the night before, which he never thought he should be able to do.

The next Monday a patron and well-wisher to our undertaking, sent in twenty crowns, after he had been acquainted with our circumstances; and another person sent likewise twenty crowns more. Besides, the above-mentioned patron, who had presented the hospital with a waggon-load of corn, sent afterwards another; and some small sums of money also came in, whereby we were carried through out difficulties for that time, till I received your letter, with a ducat inclosed in it, sent by some friend of your's unknown to me.

And these instances I was willing here to set down, that I might give you some idea of our exercise in time of probation; though I am sufficiently convinced, that narratives of this kind will seem over-simple and fanciful to the great wits of the age.

Others have, for want of better judgment, thus expressed themselves: "It was no great prize to build an house, when he received enough to do it withal: if we had such incomes, we should not think it hard to provide likewise for so many people, erect an hospital, &c." But to this I say, that they who reason thus, have no right apprehensions of the matter, supposing that I do ascribe to myself the feeding of so many people, and setting up an hospital. Whereas, if ever such a thought should insinuate itself into my mind, I should take it indeed for a temptation of the devil, and would fight against it to the utmost of my power.

The LORD hath carried me through many untrodden ways, which human reason had never been able to beat through, and hereby hath experimentally taught me the true meaning of the words of the Psalmist: *The eyes of all wait upon thee, O* LORD, *and thou givest them their meat in due season. Thou openest thine hand, and satisfiest the desire of every living thing.* And of that expression of our Saviour: *Man shall not live by bread alone, but by every word that proceedeth out of the mouth of* GOD.

And how is it possible, that seeing two hundred persons dining and supping daily in the hospital, I should make such a horrid blunder, as presumptuously to say, "'Tis I provide for all these." I protest before the LORD, that I take the whole undertaking for a work *intirely* belonging to GOD, being the product of his goodness, wherein no body ought to have any the least regard to me, since I never pretended at all to have any share in the praises redounding thence. And how soon might the LORD cut off any such selfish pretence, if I should offer to arrogate any thing to myself in this affair, by leaving me but once to myself, in passing through so many various trials, as he hitherto hath been pleased to permit to fall upon me, and through which he has wonderfully conducted me: for so, all my endeavors and hopes must be shamefully disappointed.

But as for the objection above mentioned, I say farther, that I never knew before-hand *whence* I should be supplied, nor with *what* sums: and consequently, that it is impossible for us always to make our expences exactly answer our income, which is so uncertain. The last instance may sufficiently shew what straits I find myself now and then reduced to, insomuch that there is not one crown, nay, nor one groat left: and this happens sometimes at such a time as requires a speedy relief, under very pressing circumstances. So that I must place all my confidence in a comfortable expectation of the further emanations of the inexhaustible foundation of Divine Goodness.

It seems not so difficult for a man to have recourse to GOD, under the concern of providing a maintenance for his wife and children, since herein he may with more right, and greater boldness, lay claim to his fatherly Providence. For these are nearer related to us than the children of others; to the outward maintenance of whom, no human law compelleth us. Here one might more easily say, in his applications to the LORD, "LORD, thou hast bestowed them upon me, and I hope thou wilt also take care of them." And yet we observe daily, how prone people are to overcharge their hearts with a world of vexatious cares, whenever they do not see a present stock to provide for their natural relations. All which should inspire us with an hearty sense of the hand of GOD in this undertaking, and cause us not to grudge the praises due to Him on this behalf.

But farther, I am convinced, that the presumption of any one, that should have the boldness to undertake such a work only at a venture, and upon a conceit of his own ability, to tempt the Providence of GOD, would soon cast him down headlong into the bottom of dangerous precipices, and dash in pieces the towering contrivances of his self-conceited wisdom. And this would experimentally teach him, that the *actual carrying on* of a business, was very different from the idle notions, and whimsical ideas he had framed to himself about it, whilst he beheld his *projected* enterprize at a distance. Which unexpected disappointment, I am sure, would soon check his audacious attempt, and make him give over the business, whenever he happened to be led away into some labyrinth of difficulty, where he might learn, how shallow a foundation it was to trust in human supports, which too often leave them in the lurch, that over-eagerly hunt after them; partly by reason of the backwardness the creature has to support its fellow creatures, and partly by reason of the utter impotency the creature lieth under, being unable to do any good, till the

LORD inspireth it with good thoughts to promote the cause of CHRIST, and the common good. Now, if notwithstanding the intricacy and pressure of these difficult circumstances, such an one was dunned and called upon all the day long, to supply such a numerous family, with bread, cloaths, and many other things, it would put a sudden end to all his *aerial projects*, which were so easily formed, and so far extended at the time of their contrivance; and then this question might be put to him, "Where is now thy boasting?" Such a juncture of affairs would read him a most convincing lecture, that *Faith* was not the work of human invention, but intirely of the power of GOD, and consequently that it was the greatest foolishness to ascribe to himself these things, the beginning, progress, and success whereof, depend intirely upon the aid and support of Divine Grace: which would undoubtedly then depart from the creature, as soon as it offered to grasp into its own possession, what of right belongeth only to GOD; rather glorying in the flesh, than in the LORD.

It is not my design in the least to obstruct hereby the work of faith in others. I wish rather with all my heart, that every one may, with a full assurance, and unshaken firmness of mind, trust in the living GOD, and so bring forth fruits of righteousness in greater plenty.

But this I say, let every one be sure of the foundation he builds on. Let him beware of all manner of presumptuous self-conceitedness, and of all *selfish* willing and working, even in such projects as seem directly to tend to the promotion of the good cause. He is to *count the cost* over and over: I mean, he is to make the strictest enquiry into the certainty of his call, or the moving principle he acteth upon, for fear of falling under the just censure of that proverb, *This man* (and so not the LORD) *began to build, but is not able to finish.*

For my part, I readily confess that I have been engaged in this affair, and am hardly able to give any sufficient reason for it. It was, I think, a secret guidance of the LORD, whereby I was carried to the performing of such things, as tended to an end I had not yet conceived in my mind, which inclined me afterwards to frame such a design, whereof at first I had not entertained any premeditated project; which being once laid down, it became a means, under the Divine Conduct, of carrying on, facilitating, and accomplishing the whole undertaking: and indeed the experience requisite for such a work, grew up along with the work itself. And I must needs say, that if the LORD had furnished me, when I first went about it, with all that money at once, which he hath been pleased from time to time to bestow upon me, I should never have laid it out so well, as I hope I have done, now that it hath been given us successively, and at such times when our wants did lie sensibly upon us. Such a vast sum of money, to the management whereof I never was used in my life, would have been a greater burthen to me, (if I should have been obliged to contrive, how to carry on such an undertaking with so large a stock) than all the trials I hitherto have passed through. Praised be therefore the wisdom of GOD, for all, and in all his wonderful dealings.

If any body shall offer to brand me with self-interest in this affair, I can easily bear with that aspersion; and so much the more easily, if he be of the number of those who know nothing of the trials I have undergone, since I have been engaged therein. But more especially, if he do not know that I have found greater riches in a living faith in GOD, both for me, and my relations, than emperors and kings could ever bestow upon us. The LORD hath graciously taught me how to understand, in the light of faith, the meaning of that saying, *Rom.* viii. 32. *He that spared not his own* SON, *but delivered Him up for us all, how shall He not with Him also freely give us all things?* And of that of Deut. x. 9. *Levi hath no part nor inheritance with his brethren: the* LORD *is his inheritance, according as the* LORD *thy* GOD *promised him.* I know how much is to be referred to the shadow of the old covenant in this passage; but a mortified self-denying life, becoming the true disciple of CHRIST, and consisting in a generous desertion of all they have, is more properly to be referred to the body and substance, than to the shadow and types of the law; the LORD having promised Himself to be their portion. But he that never had any experimental taste of these promises, *viz.* that he whose portion is the LORD, wanteth nothing, and that he never is a loser, that leaveth all for His sake; such a one will hardly be persuaded to lay aside his jealous surmises, because he judgeth others by himself.

But I find myself, much honored friend, swerving a little by this digression from prosecuting the account I had begun. I must then let you know farther, that the LORD, after the aforesaid trials, hath conducted us, by a gentle pace, to the end of the year 1701. Since I received the ducat of C. a benefactor sent four ducats; and another, fifty crowns; and a certain ambassador from N. forty more. Out of the before-mentioned silver mine also came in two crowns. Moreover, an unknown person sent eight bushels of corn; and the person who engaged to furnish the hospital with salt, sent in a quantity thereof. A certain minister in another province, had within his parsonage gathered a free *collection* for our hospital, amounting to forty-one crowns one shilling, which he sent in. The forementioned patron, who had used every new year to bestow fifty crowns upon the hospital, sent them now in before the old year was out: and another of our benefactors sent two hundred crowns: also a certain prince gave thirty. Not now to mention others, for brevity's sake; which yet are not forgotten before the LORD, or in my heart.

Last Christmas our children were treated by a patron, who ordered roast meat, and white bread, to be provided for them; which made them a very handsome entertainment.

Besides those benefits which have been annually gathered in this year, GOD hath excited some to bequeath in their last wills and testaments several hundreds of crowns to the hospital, which the LORD we hope will render forthcoming thereto in *his time*. One also who received a small legacy, left him by a deceased friend, presented thereof fourteen crowns to the hospital. There has likewise been sent some shifts and caps, ready made, with neckcloths, and other things of that nature. A countess sent one hundred and fourteen pounds of butter, and an hundred and six pounds of cheese. A minister sent flax and linen, with advice, that a piece of ground was sown with flax, for the use of the hospital. A certain royal officer presented to the hospital half an hundred weight of fish, and at another time an hog: and some other persons gave some beef for the benefit of the poor.

I forbear to mention all the small sums of money falling in now and then, not only because it is not for my purpose at present, (which is to give but *some* discovery of the gracious dealings, and *Providential Footsteps*, of our great GOD, for which that may suffice which has been said already upon this subject) but also because I am obliged to give a particular account only to the LORD, who hath intrusted me with the management of this affair; to whose disposal both our income and expences are intirely committed. In the mean time, I protest that I do not despise the gift of any, let it be never so *small*; because I, on one hand, keep my eyes fixed on Him who inclineth the heart, and, on the other, on the inward principle of that sincere and cordial affection, whence such charitable emanations are derived; so that now and then a few *groats* are as necessary and acceptable, as hundreds of *crowns* at some other times. As for instance, when once a poor servant, knowing nothing of the great want I was then just reduced to, offered me two crowns, being the product of her daily labor, and presented it to the hospital, as a sacrifice of her sincere charity, to be spent for the poor. And when, at another time, a well-inclined friend, coming from a journey, offered me a crown, which was given him by the way, for the hospital. Such, and the like little sums, falling in at seasonable hours, have often left as deep an impression of GOD's tender Providence upon my mind, as, at another time, most considerable supplies. The LORD be the *exceeding great reward* of all those who have cast in something for our support, in that day wherein every one shall reap the fruit of his works, whether they be good or evil.

I cannot forbear to mention here by the way, the *Cabinet of Rarities*, which, for the benefit of our pupils, at first began to be erected upon some free gifts of certain benefactors, and is since increased to a pretty good number of fine and curious pieces of *nature* and *art*.

A CONTINUATION OF THE ACCOUNT

In the mean time, the building of the hospital itself was advanced about Easter 1701, to such a degree, that the three principal stories were made habitable and useful. After this the ground floor was got ready for the apothecary's shop, and the printing-house; the former whereof was actually set up there in the beginning of the summer, and the latter, about the beginning of autumn, and both of them, thanks be to GOD, are now in a pretty good state. The laboratory belonging to the apothecary's shop, or dispensary, was erected in the yard.

The uppermost parts of the new building were finished, the chimnies perfected, and the stoves set up in their places, about the same time. The old house, which was bought in 1698, (formerly an inn) has been joined to the new house, and so fitted up for a dwelling-place and a school for the girls, as the new house contains the lodgings and school for the boys, which greatly facilitates our inspection of the schools, and the order observed therein.

This good step which has been made towards the finishing of the building, has also proved a means to use the children to a more regular practice of handy-craft traders, which hitherto was not so practicable, by reason of the several hired houses the children were lodged in. However, the progress made therein is but little as yet; and the best method we have hitherto found of putting it in motion, is by exercising the *knitting trade*; a master whereof is actually taken in. The children are made to apply themselves to it, with this difference, that some of them work more hours when they are at it, than others. Now that which is required of the knitting-master consists, at this time, in the following particulars:

1. That he come in the morning about seven o'clock, and go away at night about the same hour.

2. That he divide the wool into three sorts; the best whereof is to be used for such stockings as are to be sold; the middle sort, to make the children stockings; and the coarsest, either for gloves to the children, or to line their waistcoats, or for some other use.

3. That he have always wool made ready for working, before that be spent which they are about, and take care that the wool be well carded and dressed, as also well spun. But in this last, the children have not yet made any considerable progress, for as much as it requires a long practice to make one dextrous at it.

4. That when he receives of children what they have spun, he weigh it, and keep every one's worsted by itself, and give notice to the tutor, whether the children have performed their task as they ought to do, or not, that the task of every one being marked down in a book appointed for that purpose, such as have been idle may be rebuked.

5. That he at once weigh off so much worsted to a boy, as is required for a pair of stockings, which the boy is to keep till the stockings are done, and

when he has got them ready, the master is to weigh the stockings again, to see whether all the worsted has been used, or whether the boy has wasted any of it.

6. That he take a more particular care of about half a dozen boys, to make them perfect in knitting within the space of a month, or six weeks; yet so as not to overlook the rest.

Now as the LORD hitherto hath accompanied these small endeavors with his blessing, so I cannot forbear to mention still another particular; which is, the setting up of our *bookseller's shop*; whereby he hath given us a fresh instance that He is able to accomplish the work which he hath begun. For when, about four years ago, a sermon concerning the *Duties of Christians towards the Poor*, was published, and we had no thoughts of setting up a bookseller's shop, Providence was pleased to make this the occasion thereof, and actually to teach the person who was employed about the printing that discourse, what was his particular duty towards the poor, to be afterwards performed. And indeed he hath carried it on to this day, out of a tender regard towards them, being now fully intrusted with the management both of the bookseller's shop and the printing-house.

Afterwards it fell out, that another sermon, treating upon the *Justification of a Sinner before GOD*, was put out at the request of some friends; wherein the hidden designs of Divine Providence were soon after discovered; for this proved the beginning of a whole *set* of sermons, which were successively published, upon all the Gospels read in the Church throughout the whole year.

Before half these sermons were published, his Prussian Majesty was graciously pleased to confer the privilege of setting up both a *bookseller's shop* and a *printing-house*. However, at that time, either of them was as yet out of our reach, both for want of money requisite for such an undertaking, and of persons duly qualified for managing and carrying on the same. But, for all that, we had good hopes that the LORD would bring it to bear, in its appointed time.

In the mean while, the aforesaid person, who first set about this work, pursued it constantly, and, within a short space of time, pushed it on so far, that he wanted more hands to assist him. When this came to be known, some persons, out of a principle of self-interest, did their utmost to put a stop to it; but the LORD, who had laid the foundation, was able enough to protect it, and bring it to a full settlement, which many have wondered at.

It proved a powerful help to this undertaking, when Dr. Spener, out of a tender concern for the hospital, granted us permission to print his Paraphrase on the first epistle of *John*, and to make over to the hospital the benefit resulting from thence: which afterwards was followed with his *Responsa Theologica*, making up four volumes in quarto.

A CONTINUATION OF THE ACCOUNT

The aforesaid treatise on the first epistle of *John*, was printed in the year 1699, about Easter; in exchange for several copies whereof, we received some other books, at the yearly fair of Leipsick, kept about this time; being now fully resolved to furnish our shop with a good stock of books, which other booksellers offered for ours.

We hired a single room for this affair at first, but soon finding it too small, we were obliged to take in others that were larger, till at last it was quite removed into the new hospital, and fixed in a room particularly appointed for it, which was done August 2, 1700; where it has been kept ever since under GOD's blessing to this day.

But the overflowing corruption of this age being also crept into the bookseller's shop, by means of abundance of scandalous pamphlets, the scribblers and sellers whereof have, in these *latter times*, too much pestered the world, we soon observed that the selling and dispersing of such books, would not only draw a dreadful curse after it, but charge also the hospital with the sins of all that should buy such books, (reading whereof generally gives a lasting tincture of many impure notions, being stuffed with nothing but foolish evaporations of an idle brain) we industriously avoided all such papers or pamphlets as were accommodated to the corrupt palate of the age. And if perhaps one or two of them were brought in with other books, they were no sooner discovered than committed to the flames.

Out of the same principle, we have laid aside that sinful custom of over-rating our books, now too much grown into fashion; and, according to our Saviour's doctrine, *Yea* hath been *yea*, and *Nay, nay*, with us. As the honor of GOD, and the edification of our fellow creatures, is the very mark we hitherto have endeavored to keep our eyes fixed on, so we have done our utmost to direct our projects to this main scope; and accordingly, besides a German *Bible*, have published other such books as might answer this great end: a catalogue of the chief whereof I think fit here to annex.

Arnold's, Gottfried, Lives of the Fathers. 4to.[24]
—— Character of a Minister of the Gospel; taken out of the writings of the holy fathers, and according to the sense of the primitive church. 8vo.

------

[24] The abbreviations 4to., 8vo., and 12mo. refer to quarto, octavo, and duodecimo, which were trim sizes of print volumes, listed from largest to smallest.

Many of the titles given here were directly translated from German and thus do not represent the *English* title of any printed work. For the existing documents by and about Francke, including many that remain unpublished, visit the Francke Portal at http://digital.francke-halle.de/fsfp

Barnabas and *Clement*'s Epistles, done into High Dutch. 12mo.[25]

Benthem's present State of the Church of England. 8vo.

Boehmer's Jus Parochiale. 4to.

Erasmus's Miles Christianus. 8vo.

Franck's, *August Herman*, Set of Sunday Sermons upon the Gospels. 4to.

——— Funeral Sermon, preached at the interment of Madam Stryke.

——— Account of the Rise and Progress of the Hospital at Glaucha without Hall; discovering the most remarkable Footsteps of Divine Providence in the erecting and managing the same. 4to.

Franck's Treatise concerning the Sin of Human Fearfulness. 12mo.

——— Essay upon the Manner of CHRIST's being the Substance of the whole Scripture. With an Appendix, wherein, by way of application, is shewn, how the doctrine of CHRIST's resurrection has been pointed at in many types of the Old Testament. 8vo.

——— Essay on Education of Children to Piety and Christian Prudence. 4to.

——— The same Subject of Education considered, in a Preface prefixed to the Archbishop of Cambray's

---

25 The epistles of Barnabas and Clement rank among the earliest Christian documents outside the New Testament canon, and Barnabas' epistle is even included *after* the New Testament canon in Codex Sinaiticus.

Treatise concerning the Education of Daughters. 12mo.

—— Manductio ad Lectionem Scripturæ. Una cum Additamentis Regulas Hermeneuticas de Affectibus, & Enarrationes ac Introductiones succinctas in aliquot Epistolas Paulinas complectentibus. 12mo.

—— Some plain and short Directions concerning the true practical reading of the Bible. 12mo.

—— Introduction to the Bible, especially the New Testament; wherein more particularly the *Scope* of every book of the New Testament is laid open. Together with an Appendix, containing the substance of the treatise, reduced to a form of easy questions and answers, in order to be taught to children. Fitted for the use of schoolmasters, students in divinity, and such as are employed in catechising. 12mo.

Franck's Scheme, containing both the duty of a Minister in relation to his congregation, and the duty of the Congregation in relation of the practical improvement of the pastoral duty. More particularly concerning the right celebrating of the great Festivals, of the LORD's day, of the Apostles days, of fast days, of Lent. Likewise the repeating of sermons, the cetechetical exercises, the week sermons and lectures, the duty of prayers, and, generally, the right and saving application of the Word of God. Printed heretofore under the title of

A Memorial for Glaucha, and suited to the state of his congregation, wherein it was, about the year 1693.

—— Character of Timothy, drawn up and unfolded for the imitation of all students in divinity. 12mo.

—— Meditation upon *Grace* and *Truth*; John i. 17. wherein the true scriptural notion of these words (containing summarily the fundamental points of Christian religion) is enquired into: shewing withal how a Christian, from a lively and experimental knowledge thereof, may draw comfort and virtue for daily growth in the inward life.

—— Some Directions concerning Conversation and Retiredness; and how a Christian may, in each of them, keep up a good conscience, and improve them to a spiritual life. 12mo.

Franck's Exhortatory Discourse to the Duty of Praises and Thanksgivings. Delivered in the newly-erected Hospital at Glaucha without Hall. 4to.

—— Two Letters to some Friends abroad; containing several particular points of Christian Religion; especially under this present dispensation. 4to.

—— An Exhortatory Discourse upon the eighty-ninth Psalm, for spiritually improving the Coronation day of his Prussian Majesty, being the 18th of January, 1701. Delivered in the Hospital at Glaucha. 4to.

—— The Order and Method of Teaching in the Collegiate School (now called *Pædagogium Regium)* erected at Glaucha. 4to.

—— Præcipua Capita quihus Pædagogium Glaucha Halense differt a perisq; Scholis Publicis, 4to.

—— Of the great Decay of Church Discipline, and the Necessity of reviving it: being a Preface prefixed before Mr. Seidel's treatise against gaming, tippling, dancing, drinking clubs, and other conventicles of that nature.

—— Essay how a Man may enter into himself, in order to retrieve a true sense of Piety: in a Preface before a treatise of a similar nature. 12mo.

Franck on what Encouragement and Edification one may draw from the Examples of the primitive Christians: in a Preface before Dr. Weller's Martyr Book. 8vo.

—— Of a deceitful Conversion, upon the words in *Hosea* vii. 16. In a Preface to Mr. Wiegleb's Treatise about the right use of Luther's Catechism.

—— Essay upon Luther's High Dutch Translation of the Bible; wherein, by a collection of many passages compared with the original text, is *modestly* shewn that this version wants to be refined. 4to.

—— Apologetical Pieces concerning the aforegoing subject, and some false imputations and innovations charged upon the author.

—— Treatise upon the Duty of Prayer; whereto, by way of an Appendix, is annexed a *Reponsum*

Theologicum, or determination of the divines of the university of Kiel, in Holsatia, about the certainty of GOD's gracious granting what one prays for. Occasioned by a remarkable case of a man, who, by his prayers, cured many persons lying dangerously ill. An account whereof is given at large, and the aforesaid *Responsum Theologicum* about such extraordinary gifts subjoined, with approbation of the persons concerned therein.

—— The Love Theology; or the Life and Works of Catherine of Genoa, done out of Mr. Poiret's French edition. 12mo.

Kaepken's, Balthasar, Mystical Divinity; with Dr. Spener's Preface. 8vo.

—— Treatise of new Obedience. 8vo.

Michaelis, Joh. Henric. Tractat. de Accentibus Ebraicis. 8vo.

Petersen's, Joh. Will. Scriptural Catechism. 12mo.

Petersen's, Jane Eleonore, Spiritual Combat; unfolding the nature of this combat, the difficulties, impediments, doubts, and other practical points; set forth under the emblem of the seven churches, mentioned by St. John in the Revelation, and their several dispositions *mystically* or *internally* applied. 12mo.

Regius, Urbanus, CHRIST's Discourse with his two Disciples, in his way to Emmaus, paraphrased. 8vo.

Spener's, Philip James, Paraphrase on the first epistle of John. 4to.

—— Responsa Theologica, 4 tom. 4to.
Strykius, Samuel, De Cautelis Testamentorum. Lat.
  4to.
Vackerod's, Gottfried, Enquiry into the nature of things
  commonly called *indifferent*; against Mr. Roth. 4to.
—— Victory of Truth; against the same.
Wiegleb's, Jerome, Treatise upon the chief Hindrances
  in the Work of Conversion. 12mo.

July the 28th, the LORD gave us a fresh proof of
his favor herein towards the hospital; for while we
were concerned about the necessaries for putting
the press in order, we met with a good opportunity
of purchasing both letters and other utensils.

In ordering this affair, we were taken up till
Michaelmas, and then a compositor, and some other
workmen, were actually employed; and since that
time, *two presses* have been always kept going.

Likewise some of the boys bred in the hospital,
have been employed in learning this trade, whereby
in time they may get an honest livelihood.

This now proved a powerful support for a
bookseller's shop: for having employed hitherto
several presses in Hall, or some other places, we
have met with many disappointments, which are
now, by so regular a settlement, happily prevented,
and every thing relating to the hospital rendered
effectual, by the joint concurrence of all these
establishments.

A CONTINUATION OF THE ACCOUNT

No less hath been the advantage derived to the hospital by means of the *apothecary's shop*; so that we are utterly unable to make a return of thanks suitable to the benefits we have received at the hand of GOD. Mention hath been made already, in the foregoing narrative, what hard circumstances we lay under, on account of the sick and diseased in the hospital, and how the LORD succoured us in so sad a juncture, by providing us with a specific, called *Elixir Polychrestum*, against the burning and malignant fever, which then raged in our hospital.

Soon after another medicine came to our hand, called *Magisterium Diaphoreticum*, being very useful to carry off the scabby and scurvy eruptions, and other distempers of that nature, incident to hospitals; which has this particular virtue, that although it procures a large sweat to the patient, yet it doth not in the least diminish his strength, but rather refresh and revive the spirits. It is also useful in fevers, tooth-ach, apostemes, and for destroying of worms.

But the Providence of the LORD was more eminently discovered in another medicine, called *Essentia Dulcis*, by the use whereof many persons, who were almost spent under several languishing distempers, have been happily restored, and after their recovery, excited to praise and extol the Name of GOD. And although this medicine doth not properly belong to the apothecary's shop, it being, as well as some few others, prepared apart by the physician himself, in a laboratory, yet he furnisheth the apothecary's shop therewith; and whatever we get by it, is intirely laid out for the use of the hospital, and other distressed persons; a great many people having already enjoyed the benefit thereof, even without the walls of the hospital.

For instance, a gentlewoman being under a grievous distemper, and constantly confined to her bed for seven years, was almost spent with ulcers, both internal and external, shewing themselves almost every month, and causing the most furious pains: her breast was very much disordered, and this attended with other dismal accidents; for her back-bone was, by the lasting violence of the distemper, become crooked, and one of her arms, and one of her legs, were the breadth of two fingers shorter than their opposites. This sad and violent distemper was at last conquered by the use of this medicine; so that, under GOD's blessing, she was not only set free from her raging pain, but her contracted limbs were so far extended in one night, that they regained their just proportion, and her back-bone was likewise restored to its natural state, so that now she is able to go without help.

It has likewise been observed, that this *Essentia Dulcis* cheereth up nature, promotes rest and sleep, and consequently is very useful for old and decayed people. It has a special effect upon the stone and gravel; an instance whereof has been seen in a person, affected therewith to such a degree, that he resolved to submit to the painful operation of cutting, being scarce able to stir or help himself at all; but by the use of this medicine, he was restored so far, that he could either walk on foot, or endure the shaking of a coach. Not now to mention its other signal effects, in curing the gout, palpitations of the heart, falling sickness,[26] the cholic and convulsions, weakness of the sight, and the like.

The surgeons have found it very serviceable in *cancers*, and other ulcers which seemed to be incurable. It has also restored withered limbs to their former vigor and proportion, being only outwardly anointed therewith. Those that are constant laborers in our hospital, have reaped no small benefit by it, and I myself have reason to praise the LORD for the effect it has had upon me; it being of such a nature that it reviveth the strength and vigor of the body tired out by hard work. But a particular paper being printed, setting forth more at large the virtues of this medicine, I forbear at present to mention any more of it.

It would require too prolix a narrative, if I should give an account in particular, of every step of Divine Providence, especially how the LORD hath inclined the heart of many eminent persons to join their endeavors for supporting the undertaking, after it was begun. Amongst others, he hath been pleased to excite a well-disposed physician to communicate to the hospital some his *Arcana Medica*, which he by

---

[26] That is, epilepsy. (M.S.)

experience has found extraordinary useful [*sic*] in most desperate cases. All which make us hope that the LORD will farther enable us, even in this point, the more effectually to support all manner of poor and distressed people.

After this account I have given you, most honored friend, of the several blessings which hitherto we have met with in erecting the bookseller's and apothecary's shop, you may possibly be apt to think that, under such circumstances as I have been describing, the hospital might in great part be maintained by the products of these *two foundations*, and so you may wonder at such hard trials as have been mentioned before. But to undeceive you in this affair, you must know, that the carrying on of these several establishments (tending to a future support of the undertaking) has hitherto rather increased, than lessened the difficulties. It is true, that whensoever the wheels of these several constitutions shall be all set a-going, and the children have arrived to some perfection in the management of their work, this may prove, in all appearance, a powerful support for the hospital, and so satisfy at last that unbelieving and wavering sort of people, which hitherto have doubted so much of the success of the affair, because there was no fixed fund provided for it. But so long as these things are not brought to a firm and settled state, (especially there being no more money provided for establishing these, and carrying them on, than for the hospital itself) any rational man may easily conclude, that the hospital cannot reap as yet any benefit from them. But I must needs say, that even this I take for one of the most eminent steps the wonderful Providence of GOD hitherto hath traced out before us, *viz.* that for the settling of these constitutions, we have had no other fund than we had for erecting the hospital itself, which was only the propitious Providence and goodness of GOD.

After we had thus been convinced, by many proofs, of GOD's tender regard to the poor, we resolved then to promote, under his blessing, the four following things, which in time to come may prove instrumental to the facilitating this business, *viz.* 1. The *bookseller's shop.* 2. The privilege of a *printing-house.* 3. The *apothecary's shop.* 4. The *children's constant work.* From whence it may sufficiently appear, that these particular undertaking have been no less attended with frequent trials, than the setting up the hospital itself, and which were only to be conquered by prayer, and faith in the LORD; so that the laying down a particular account of all the circumstances of these several foundations, would take up too much time. In short, necessity itself has taught us, that whatsoever money is gained by these means, ought not to be laid out for any other use, but to be intirely employed in improving that stock from whence it sprung, unless we would see a sudden decay thereof.

By this so large account of the hospital, you, my most honored friend, may perhaps be inclined to imagine, that my thoughts must needs be employed in, and hurried about with the management of every branch thereof, and consequently too much distracted, and so hindered in the discharge of my pastoral office. But I have already said, in the foregoing account, that *every branch* has a particular, and that a faithful *overseer*, to carry it on: so that I am only concerned therein, so far as it falleth under a mutual debate, both of *them*, in their several places, and of *myself*, as the present *director*; and this is confined to an hour after supper, which, by reason of my circumstances, I could not put to any other use.

But here I cannot forbear mentioning two *obstacles*, which hitherto have given me a great deal of trouble, though I endeavor to make the best I can of such uneasy and perplexing accidents. One is, that people fancy that I am plentifully provided with ready money, laid up in store; which false supposition encourages them to make frequent addresses to me, that I would bestow some of it upon them; and sometimes they ask for pretty large sums, which some would borrow, and others beg: and this happens often at such a time, when, in all probability, they may have more money than myself.

Now though I not only lay before them the most sensible proofs, to convince them, that the refusal of their demand is not the effect of want of *charity*, but of *ability*; and also endeavor to shew them how the LORD has confined every one to certain limits of assisting his fellow creatures, beyond which he is not able to go; that so people may be refrained from idolizing creatures and human supports, instead of adoring Him who is the inexhaustible fountain of goodness; yet many will not acquiesce in such and the like demonstrations, but give way to malignant suspicions, which afterwards breed slanders, and other vices of that kind; especially when they believe such groundless reports as have been spread abroad, of the plenty of our hospital.

The other *obstacle* and *difficulty* the business lies under, is this, that several people, both from neighbouring and distant places, importune me that they may be maintained here, or received into the hospital; failing of their desired success in their respective places and vocations. And I must confess, that such circumstances have given me still a fuller discovery of the deceitfulness of men's hearts. The wonderful Providence of GOD, whereby so many have hitherto been maintained in this hospital, should prove a means to make people draw nearer to Him, who is the impartial and inexhausted Spring, from whence all the rivulets of so many endearing and ravishing proofs of Divine Mercy have sprung; and who is most ready to preserve every one's soul and body, if they will but shake off the pollutions of the world, and submit with cheerfulness to the will of GOD, under all the

179

dispensations of his Providence; and not put their trust in men, which indeed is a most abominable idolatry. But now we may observe how the heart of man takes every thing by the wrong handle, and instead of tracing out the true Well Spring by such streams as flow out from thence, is too apt to gape after some small emanations, and to acquiesce therein; though they are immediately dried up, and utterly cut off, as soon as the Fountain witholds its supply.

If one offers to rectify the notions of such persons, and to give them an insight into the most ardent and affectionate love of GOD towards them that have a sincere regard to his honor, to raise thereby in them, if possible, some reciprocal flames of love, or to inspire them with an hearty confidence in so gracious a Master, they yet remain strangers to the *power of faith*, and colour over their unbelief with these and the like expressions: "That though they had no want of trust in GOD, yet the LORD did not act without means:" not considering that GOD is also supreme Master of all *means*, able by Himself to do exceeding abundantly *above all* we ask or think; provided we mind our duty, which is to wait patiently for his help, and with constant prayer and self-denial, make our application to Him; committing ourselves to the government of his Providence, with such a resignation as becomes a creature, and child of GOD, to pay to his Creator and Father.

A CONTINUATION OF THE ACCOUNT

The LORD have mercy upon such poor people! and shew them, that so far as they cast their eyes on me, they thereby decline from the true scope of the whole undertaking; which is not in the least to set up any thing that may lessen people's dependence upon the LORD; much less that they make any thing of me; knowing well enough that I am but a poor unprofitable servant, and undone worm, if the LORD withdraw himself from me, I should be satisfied, if every one would but learn so much by my example, as to know by experience the meaning of that expression: *When this poor man cried, the* LORD *heard him, and delivered him out of all his troubles:*[27] and so rely intirely upon Him, who being the most independent Good, hath an everlasting spring within himself, and so is infinitely *able* to help. But this will teach them also, that as the LORD doth not hear sinners, they are thence bound to subdue their unbelieving hearts, and the whole bent of their corrupted nature, sincerely concerning themselves about an hearty reformation of their lives.

Whereas, most honored friend, if I should connive at such gross mistakes as I just now have mentioned, and take in all manner of people that come in my way, and even those who act upon a mere secular principle, (these being generally of a loose conversation, and very importunate, which afterwards breeds abundance of other disorders,

---

[27] Psalm 34.6.

that get too soon the ascendent over young people) nothing would ensue but a most certain catastrophe of the whole undertaking.

I think it not my duty to intrust any person with the management of any part of the hospital, except I discover in him a real sense of religion, joined with a generous resolution to renounce all carnal *bye-ends* in so important a place. And I do not engage with any that are strangers to me, nor do I recommend such to others, for fear I might defraud my neighbour with false coin, under pretence of performing the part of a friend.

Now if, notwithstanding all this circumspection which I think necessary in such a juncture, I sometimes take a false step, then I readily confess that I am but a man; yet willing to mend to my utmost such things as may be discovered to me that want reformation.

Any man that is himself concerned in the management of an undertaking of this nature, best knows the difficulties attending it; especially if one considers the *necessity* of good and faithful laborers, on one hand, and the *scarcity* of such, on the other; keeping those at a distance who make worldly gain or self-interest their aim, and so prove good for nothing, but are apt to create mischief and disorders. But he that never was himself engaged in such an affair, commonly finds the greatest fault with them who labor in it, because he hath no other idea of it, than what he frameth in his own idle fancy, without any actual experience of those things which befal such as are employed therein.

The overflowing corruption of our age is arrived to such an height, that one cannot enough lament the languishing condition religion lies under; which is the cause that in such a juncture of affairs, and under the concurrence of so various circumstances, one is not able to serve any one, without giving great offence to others, besides an uneasy and unprofitable anxiety to himself. It is indeed a work of the absolute power of GOD, to make a way through these difficulties; who yet, in the mean time, will have us rest satisfied in the present dispensation of his grace, and that we heartily endeavor to be found faithful in our station.

It often comes into my mind, that if the rich men of this world, who are so forward to hoard up treasures by thousands, and hundred thousands had but as much charity as money, it would then prove no hard matter to set up *workhouses* every where; and thereby to prevent, at least, the frivolous excuses of some, who are too apt to tell us, that no work was cut out for them, though they were never so willing to get their living thereby. Alas! how many poor ignorant souls might be rescued from the dominion of sin and Satan, and so brought back to the LORD by such, and the like, charitable institutions. But indeed it seems to me, that riches are now attended with secret judgments of GOD, eating out, as it were, that little satisfaction which the owners might otherwise reap from them, so that they prove a torment and daily vexation, both to them that are in pursuit after, and those that are possessed of them, who put themselves to a great deal of trouble and disquiet upon that account. Hence it is, that they fall into most violence quarrels and law-suits about an handful of money, and expose themselves to thieves and robbers, and to a number of other afflicting accidents, which usually accompany the possession of the things of this world. Whereas they might prove the means of doing much good, besides the joy and inward satisfaction that would infallibly redound to the possessors, if they managed well their riches. No sooner now are such covetous niggards dead, but the greedy inheritors of an estate, so unhappily hoarded up, will waste both themselves and their estate with pomp and superfluities. All which may give us a sufficient insight, both into the foolishness of people thus charmed with uncertain riches, and the *judgment* of GOD following at the heels of such sinful idolatry.

But doth the LORD want the help of rich and wealthy people? and is He not able to bring about his designs without them? or is He so poor that he must depend upon their support? Surely no. The truth is, that many have made themselves *unworthy* to prove instrumental in furthering so great a blessing by their riches, which indeed were given them to advance such noble and charitable undertakings, but have hitherto been misapplied by them, to satisfy the cravings of a covetous disposition. Many who pretend more than others to a sense of charity, seem often big with abundance of specious projects, which, they say, shall in their *proper season* be put in execution; but expecting such an opportunity as best suits their fancy, and so deferring those from one time to another, they at last find themselves involved in such circumstances, that they would fain be doing some good, but it being then out of their reach, all their projects and contrivances come to nothing.

Blessed therefore are those rich men which regard the Apostle's exhortation, 1 Tim. vi. 17–19. Charge them that are rich in this world, that they be not high-minded, nor trust in uncertain riches, but in the living GOD, who giveth us richly all things to enjoy. That they do good, that they be rich in good works, ready to distribute, willing to communicate. Laying up in store for themselves a good foundation against the time to come, that they may lay hold on eternal life.

Such are the judgments of GOD, now overflowing the world with an inundation of so dreadful disorders, being the just effects of our sins! Yet the LORD is able to help when, how, and by what means he pleaseth. Let us therefore intirely rely upon Him, who standeth in need of no man's help to support him, and yet hath the hearts of all men in his hand, to incline them which way he pleaseth. Each of us shall in due time reap what he hath sown here, whether sparingly or bountifully.

But I must mention one thing more before I conclude, which is, that besides such concerns as more nearly relate to the hospital, we have also kept up, under GOD's blessing, a *constitution* begun for the benefit of such as beg from door to door, and either live here in town, or come from other places. Two hours are set apart every day, one in the forenoon, another in the afternoon, wherein these poor people are first instructed in the principles of religion, and afterwards relieved with a supply of their temporal wants.

Likewise the hospital for the maintenance of a few poor *widows*, depending, under GOD, upon the generous charity of one particular well-disposed gentleman, hath continued hitherto in a flourishing condition.

The rest of our institutions that have been hitherto carried on, to retrieve, if possible, a good education, I here pass by in silence, because they have no immediate relation to the hospital, to give an account whereof was at present my only design. If any body be desirous to inform himself of the nature of our *Pædagogium*, or collegiate school, I refer him to a *large account*, wherein the whole *method* of managing that affair is distinctly laid down.[28] As likewise another small treatise has been published,

---

[28] *Ordnung und Lehr-Art, wie selbige in dem Paedagogio zu Glaucha an Halle eingeführet ist.* 1702.

about inculcating upon children *good Principles both of Religion and Christian Prudence.*[29]

I cannot forbear mentioning here also the *prevailing example*, which is shewn us by many well-disposed persons in England, who after having formed themselves into *several societies*, have set up, and hitherto successfully maintained, abundance of charity-schools; opposed and discouraged vice, introduced some degree of catechising ignorant people, published many useful books, and by other laudable projects, given encouragement to other nations. Which makes me hope, that they also begin to think it time to concern themselves something more for the *life* of religion, and *power* of godliness; chusing rather to promote the same by vigorously carrying on such *practical methods* as strike at the root of vice and profaneness, than by maintaining unnecessary and unprofitable disputes.

Besides these and the like encouragements I have hitherto met with, the LORD hath given me one proof more of his goodness, which is, the joining to me another sincere *fellow-laborer*, who, together with him that hath been with me these many years, beareth no small part of the pastoral care; by which means a larger opportunity is confered on me, to prosecute some other things tending to the common good. I have already gained so much time hereby, as

---

[29] *Unterricht, wie die Kinder zur wahren Gottseligkeit und Christlichen Klugheit sollen angeführet werden.* 1702.

to give the finishing stroke to a treatise, intitled, *NICODEMUS*; treating upon the *unlawfulness of Fear before Men*; which being about half done some years ago, was laid aside by the intervention of other affairs:[30] and to publish another, setting forth CHRIST *as the Substance of the whole Scripture.*[31]

And thus I think, most honored friend, I have at present answered your expectation, in giving some account of the most *remarkable passages* of Divine Providence that have hitherto befallen us in the management of the hospital; intirely refering the communication of this letter to your prudence; but reserving to myself the care of putting it out here in print, as a *Continuation* of that *Narrative* which has been already set forth. The LORD hath not been pleased as yet to make us known to one another by sight; yet I assure you that your letters, discovering your faith in, and your love to *JESUS CHRIST* and all mankind, prove no small excitement to me, and which I hope have been effectual to the uniting our

[30] *Nicodemus oder Tractätlein von der Menschenfurcht.* 1701. This tract was translated and abridged by John Wesley and printed in 1749 under the title *Nicodemus, or a Treatise on the Fear of Man.* (M.S.)

[31] *Christus der Kern Heiliger Schrift*, 1702. Printed in English in 1732, under the title *Christus Sacrae Scripturae Nucleus: Or, Christ the Sum and Substance of All the Holy Scriptures in the Old and New Testament*, with the anonymous note, "now render'd into *English*, by an Antient Doctor of Physick". (M.S.)

hearts in a most tender sense of reciprocal love and kindness, which is a foretaste here of that eternal life, the full enjoyment whereof will follow then, when we come to be favored with endless joys before the throne of our LORD JESUS CHRIST! To whose infinite mercy I commit not only the full reward of your charitable inclination towards us, but also yourself, in this beginning of the year; praying Him to bless you both here and hereafter.

Now unto the King Eternal, Immortal, Invisible, the only wise GOD, *be honor and glory for ever and ever. Amen.*

    I remain, most honored friend,
        Your true friend to serve you,
            AUGUSTUS HERMAN FRANCK.

Glaucha without Hall,
Jan. 7, 1702.

www.ingramcontent.com/pod-product-compliance
Lightning Source LLC
Chambersburg PA
CBHW051824040426
42447CB00006B/356